THE GARDEN TOURIST.

2 0 0 1

A Guide to Gardens, Garden Tours, Shows and Special Events

LOIS G. ROSENFELD

THE GARDEN TOURIST PRESS

Published by The Garden Tourist Press
372 Hopper Avenue
Ridgewood, NJ 07450

INTRODUCTION

The **Garden Tourist**® celebrates its tenth year of publication with new regional editions, each containing more than 200 of the region's best garden happenings and dozens of wonderful gardens to visit whenever and wherever you travel.

We've added some brand new features to make your garden travels even more rewarding.

The book is now organized into two easy-to-use sections, one for the **Guide to Gardens** with listings by state, and one for **Selected Events**, listed by state, city and date. You'll find complete organization information in both sections to make it easy to reach the gardens and event sponsors.

There are new introductions to both the Guide and Events sections to give you a "taste" of the region, call your attention to special developments and highlight some of the more significant events.

We've added new **Secret Garden Guides** to destinations in the U.S. and Canada, insider tips from local writers to little known, less frequented gems that are well worth a visit.

The look of the book has changed, too, with one of the region's beautiful gardens on each front cover.

The Garden Tourist 2001 retains many of the features that readers have found so useful in prior editions.

There's a handy list of every region's major shows at the back of each edition, with our "top picks" selections of three, four and five stars right in the listings.

We've labeled dozens of events that are recommended for families. We've expanded our list of web addresses, so you can enjoy some of the best garden touring available on the worldwide web.

The **Far Away Places** section has been expanded with even more important horticultural events overseas.

Don't forget to check our web site at **www.gardentourist.com** for latest developments and updates. And please let us hear from you with your suggestions and comments.

Remember that event schedules do change, so be sure and check ahead. Happy garden touring!

CONTENTS

Guide to Gardens

Alabama	1	Puerto Rico	17
Florida	3	South Carolina	17
Georgia	7	Tennessee	19
Kentucky	10	Virgin Islands	20
Louisiana	10	Virginia	20
Mississippi	12	West Virginia	24
North Carolina	13		

Selected Events

Alabama	25	North Carolina	55
Florida	29	South Carolina	61
Georgia	41	Tennessee	65
Kentucky	48	Virgin Islands	71
Louisiana	51	Virginia	71
Mississippi	54	West Virginia	80

Far Away Places 81

Flower & Garden Shows 90

Secret Garden Guide 100

THE GARDEN TOURIST 2001

Now in Five Regional Editions

Midwest

Illinois	Michigan	North Dakota	**In Canada**
Indiana	Minnesota	Ohio	Manitoba
Iowa	Missouri	South Dakota	Ontario
Kansas	Nebraska	Wisconsin	

Northeast

Connecticut	Maryland	New York	**In Canada**
Delaware	Massachusetts	Pennsylvania	New
District of	New	Rhode Island	Brunswick
Columbia	Hampshire	Vermont	Newfoundland
Maine	New Jersey		Nova Scotia
			Quebec

Southeast

Alabama	Kentucky	Puerto Rico	Virginia
Florida	Louisiana	South Carolina	West Virginia
Georgia	Mississippi	Tennessee	
	North Carolina	Virgin Islands	

Southwest & Rockies

Arizona	Idaho	Texas	**In Canada**
Arkansas	Montana	Utah	Alberta
Colorado	New Mexico	Wyoming	Saskatchewan
	Oklahoma		

West

Alaska	Nevada	**In Canada**
California	Oregon	British
Hawaii	Washington	Columbia

To order other editions, visit your local bookstore or send payment of $12.95 plus $4 shipping and handling with order specifying edition to The Garden Tourist Press, 372 Hopper Avenue, Ridgewood, NJ 07450. *Set of all five available at a 20% discount plus $10 s&h.*
For more information, call (201)447-2331 or e-mail mktsols@idt.net.

GUIDE TO GARDENS

See also Selected Events on pages 25-80

Welcome to the Southeast

The Southeast region contains a marvelous variety of gardens, from gracious southern gardens like The Huntsville-Madison County Botanical Garden in Alabama (shown on the front cover of this edition) to tropical paradises like Fairchild in Florida and the rich piedmont flora of the Atlanta Botanical Gardens.

The region includes an array of estate gardens rich in history, like those of the fabulous Biltmore in North Carolina, Lewis Ginter in Virginia and Cheekwood in Tennessee with its fabulous collection of sculpture. The southeast also features some of the country's most unique gardens, like the huge walled garden at Riverbanks in South Carolina and the gardens of the American Rose Center in Louisiana, the country's largest rose park.

Don't forget to check Garden Tourist's Selected Events on page 25 for some of the best events in the region. You'll also find even more gardens, open on just special occasions, plus lots of garden organizations, numbers and web site addresses, so you can find out what's going on garden-wise whenever and wherever you travel.

ALABAMA
See also Events for Alabama.

Bellingrath Gardens & Home
12401 Bellingrath Gardens Road
Theodore, AL 36582
(334)973-2217
Location: 20 miles from Mobile
Web: www.bellingrath.org
❧ The Gardens comprise 65 landscaped acres with towering live oaks draped in Spanish moss. Special features include a rose garden, conservatory, great lawn, butterfly garden, rockery, formal gardens, oriental-American gardens, Mirror Lake and the Bayou Boardwalk for viewing the natural habitat and wildlife.

Birmingham Botanical Gardens
2612 Lane Park Road
Birmingham, AL 35223
(205)414-3900
Web: www.bbgardens.org
❧ The 67-acre Gardens contain over twenty display gardens including a fine Japanese garden, a tea garden, Zen garden and bonsai exhibit. The large conservatory has seasonal exhibitions and houses cacti, succulents and orchids.
Hours: Dawn-dusk
Fees: Free

Dismals Canyon
Route 3
Phil Campbell, AL
(205)993-4559

Mail: PO Box 281, Phil Campbell,
AL 35581
Web: www.dismalscanyon.com
🕸 A registered National Natural Landmark, the site features a natural arboretum of 27 different types of trees within a 100 foot radius. Other highlights include seven natural bridges, a winding stairway encased in natural rock, over 350 species of wildflowers and many miles of trails.

Donald E. Davis Arboretum
Garden Drive
Auburn, AL
(334)844-5770
Mail: 101 Rouse LSB, Auburn University, Auburn, AL 36849
🕸 Founded in 1959, the Arboretum features a collection of plants native to Alabama, including hardwoods and native vines. Under development are display areas for vegetation characteristic of Black-Belt soils, prairie, coastal bog and sand dunes.
Hours: Dawn to dusk
Fees: Free

Dothan Area Botanical Gardens
5130 Headland Avenue
Dothan, AL 36303
(334)793-3224
Web: www.dabg.com
🕸 A garden in the making, the 50-acre site encompasses partially wooded, rolling land traversed by Cedar Creek. Current features include a 400-bush rose garden, raised-bed herb garden, paved nature trails, demonstration greenhouse and reconstruction of the 100-year old tenant farmer home.
Hours: Dawn-sundown
Fees: Free

The Huntsville-Madison County Botanical Garden
4747 Bob Wallace Avenue
Huntsville, AL 35805
(256)830-4447
Web: www.hsvbg.org
🕸 The 112-acre Garden features a beautiful 5-acre central corridor planting with roses, daylilies, ferns, herbs, aquatics, flower and butterfly gardens. Other highlights include nature trails, a new Butterfly House and new Exhibit Hall. April is a good time to visit when the dogwoods, wildflowers, poppies, azaleas, tulips and pansies are in full bloom.
Hours: 9am-6:30pm Mon-Sat; 1-6:30pm Sun
Fees: $4; $3 seniors; $2 students; under 6 free

Jasmine Hill Gardens & Outdoor Museum
3001 Jasmine Hill Road
Wetumpka, AL
(334)567-6463
Location: 8 miles from Montgomery
Mail: PO Box 210792, Montgomery, AL 36121-0792
Web: www.jasminehill.org
🕸 The 20-acre Gardens feature extensive collections of camellias, Japanese cherries, azaleas and crape myrtles. Other highlights include Grecian-style statuary, fountains, native stone walks and a full-scale replica of the ruins of Temple of Hera in Olympia.
Hours: 9am-5pm Tues-Sun; closed Mon except holidays
Fees: $5; $3 children 6-12; children under 6 free

Mobile Botanical Gardens
5151 Museum Drive

Mobile, AL
(334)342-0555
Mail: PO Box 8382, Mobile, AL 36689
🏛 Located in the heart of Mobile, the
Gardens encompass 64 acres of cultivated
areas and nature trails. Highlights include
native and exotic azaleas, camellias, hollies, magnolias and ferns, a rhododendron
garden and herb garden. Peak blooming
season is late March and early April.
Hours: 8am-5pm
Fees: Free

University of Alabama Arboretum
Pelham Loop Road
Tuscaloosa, AL
(205)553-3278
Mail: PO Box 870344, Tuscaloosa, AL
35487
Web: www.uah.edu/admin/Fac/grounds/
🏛 This 60-acre Arboretum is located a few
miles from the campus and emphasizes
indigenous trees, shrubs and wildflowers.
The garden is divided into four sections:
native woodland, ornamentals, a wildflower
garden and an experimental garden.
Hours: 7am-5pm
Fees: Free

**University of Alabama in Huntsville
Arboretum**
Huntsville, AL
(256)890-6482
Mail: University of Alabama, Facilities &
Operations Building, Huntsville, AL 35899
🏛 Situated on the University's 360-acre
campus, the Arboretum contains more than
200 different deciduous trees and conifers,
with many rare specimens not commonly
seen outside of collections.
Fees: Free

FLORIDA
See also Events for Florida.

Alfred B. Maclay State Gardens
3540 Thomasville Road
Tallahassee, FL 32308
(850)487-4115
Web: www.ssnow.com/maclay/
🏛 Now a 300-acre state park, this former
estate features excellent azalea and camellia collections. The site includes formal gardens, a flowering tree collection and
demonstration camellia gardens.

Bok Tower Gardens
1151 Tower Boulevard
Lake Wales, FL 33853
(863)676-1408
Web: www.boktower.org
🏛 Designed by Frederick Law Olmsted, Jr.,
the Gardens are planted with camellias,
azaleas and magnolias, as well as an
important collection of palms. The nature
observatory affords views of birds and
wildlife around the pond.

Butterfly World
3600 West Sample Road
Coconut Creek, FL 33073
(954)977-4400
Location: 15 miles north of Ft. Lauderdale
Web: www.butterflyworld.com
🏛 The site is comprised of outdoor gardens
and five large screened aviaries, sanctuaries for thousands of butterflies. In the gardens are waterfalls, ponds and orchids.
Other highlights include a lakeside botanical garden and a large collection of passion
flowers.
Hours: 9am-5pm Mon-Sat; 1-5pm Sun;
guided butterfly tours 10am the 2nd Sat of

each month
Fees: $12.95; $7.95 children 4-12; children under 4 free

Cypress Gardens
2641 South Lake Summit Drive
Winter Haven, FL
(800)282-2123
Location: Southwest of Orlando and east of Tampa
Mail: PO Box 1, Winter Haven, FL 33884
Web: www.cypressgardens.com
🏵 Cypress Gardens is composed of more than 200 acres planted with tropical, subtropical and temperate plants.

Eden State Gardens
181 Eden Garden Road
Point Washington, FL
(850)231-4214
Location: Panama City Beach
Mail: PO Box 26, Point Washington, FL 32454
Web: www.dep.state.fl.us/parks/
🏵 Now part of Florida State Parks, the property is the former home and gardens of the lumber magnate William Henry Wesley. The moss-draped live oaks, which predate the Wesley development, dominate the lawns. From October to May camellias and azaleas are in bloom with peak bloom in March.

Edison & Ford Winter Estates
2350 McGregor Blvd
Fort Myers, FL 33901
(941)334-7419
Web: www.edison-ford-estate.com
🏵 Established by Thomas Alva Edison, the gardens comprise 14 acres of lush tropical plantings. They are home to hundreds of

varieties of plants, ranging from orchids to the unique African Hanging Sausage tree and the largest banyan tree in the continental United States.
Hours: 9am-5pm Mon-Sat; noon-5pm Sun; closed major holidays
Fees: Estate tours $12 Jan-Apr, $11 May-Dec; $5.50 children 6-12

Fairchild Tropical Garden
10901 Old Cutler Road
Coral Gables, FL 33156
(305)667-1651
Web: www.ftg.org
🏵 The 83-acre Garden displays tropical plants from around the world. Highlights include collections of palms and cycads, a botanical museum, conservatory, rain forest and a sunken garden. Narrated tram tours are available.
Hours: 9:30am-4:30pm; closed Christmas
Fees: $8; children under 13 free

Flamingo Gardens
3750 Flamingo Road
Davie/Ft. Lauderdale, FL 33330
(954)473-2955
🏵 The Gardens are home to one of the largest collections of heliconias, as well as the largest group of champion trees in the country - twenty-one in all. Highlights include the rain forest, Everglades and citrus groves.

Florida Tech Botanical Garden
150 West University Blvd
Melbourne, FL 32901
(407)768-8086
🏵 The 30-acre site is a natural preserve of different habitats, from sandy uplands of

pines and palmettos to the lush hammock of oaks, maples, hickories and other hardwoods. It's accessible from paths on the outskirts of the Florida Tech campus or from the campus.
Hours: 8am-6pm
Fees: Free

Fruit & Spice Park
24801 SW 187th Avenue
Homestead, FL 33031
(305)247-5727
Location: 35 miles south of Miami
Web: www.co.miami-dade.fl.us/parks/fruitandspice.htm
🌱 Established in 1944 by the Miami-Dade Park and Recreation Department, the 32-acre Park is internationally known for its more than 500 varieties of exotic and sub-tropical fruit, nut, spice and herb trees and shrubs.
Hours: 10am-5pm daily; closed Christmas
Fees: $3.50; $1 children 12 and under

Harry P. Leu Gardens
1920 North Forest Avenue
Orlando, FL 32803
(407)246-2620
Web: www.leugardens.org
🌱 Located in the historic district at the heart of Orlando, this 50-acre site features camellias, roses, palms and tropical plants. Leu House Museum, dating from the 1880s, is listed on the National Register of Historic Places.
Hours: Winter 9am-5pm; Daylight Savings Time 9am-8pm Mon-Sat, 9am-6pm Sun
Fees: $4; $1 children

Heathcote Botanical Gardens
210 Savannah Road
Fort Pierce, FL 34982
(561)464-4672
Location: 50 miles from West Palm Beach
🌱 Begun in 1985 as a conservation project, the 3.5-acre site is still under development. It offers several specialized gardens including a Japanese garden, palm walk and both native and exotic subtropical flowers and foliage.
Hours: Year round 9am-5pm Tues-Sat; Nov-Apr 1-5pm Sun
Fees: $3; $1 children 6-12; children under 6 free

The Kampong
4013 Douglas Road
Coconut Grove, FL 33133
(305)442-7169
Location: 4 miles south of downtown Miami
Web: www.ntbg.org
🌱 Administered by the National Tropical Botanical Garden, the 9-acre Garden includes a variety of tropical plantings.

Kanapaha Botanical Gardens
4700 SW 58th Drive
Gainesville, FL 32608
(352)372-4981
Web: hammock.ifas.ufl.edu/kanapaha
🌱 The 62-acre site contains many specialty gardens, including a butterfly garden, spring flower garden, palm hammock collection, Florida's largest public bamboo garden, a vinery, as well as hummingbird, rock, herb, bog and sunken gardens.

Marie Selby Botanical Gardens
811 South Palm Avenue

Sarasota, FL 34236
(941)366-5731
Web: www.selby.org
🌺 The 12-acre site is perhaps best known for its collection of more than 6,000 orchids. Other highlights include seven greenhouses, a botanical museum and twenty distinct garden areas, ranging from bamboo and banyans to butterfly-attracting plants and bromeliads.
Hours: 10am-5pm
Fees: $8; $4 children 6-11; under 6 free

McKee Botanical Garden
350 South US Highway 1
Vero Beach, FL 32962
(561)794-0601
Web: www.mckeegarden.org
🌺 Scheduled to reopen in March 2001, the 18-acre Garden is a major restoration project of the Indian River Land Trust. Formerly McKee Jungle Gardens, it is one of the oldest botanical gardens in Florida and has become famous for its water lily and orchid collections.
Hours: Scheduled to open in 2001; current tours by appointment only

Mounts Botanical Garden
531 North Military Trail
West Palm Beach, FL 33415
(561)233-1749
Web: www.mounts.org
🌺 Palm Beach County's oldest and largest garden, this 13-acre site is home to a variety of tropical and subtropical plants. It contains exotic trees, a rain forest, tropical fruit collection, Florida native plants, rose, butterfly, water and vegetable gardens.

Pan's Garden
386 Hibiscus Avenue
Palm Beach, FL
(561)832-0731
Directions: Worth Avenue in downtown Palm Beach
Mail: Preservation Foundation of Palm Beach, 356 South County Road, Palm Beach, FL 33480
🌺 Located in the heart of downtown Palm Beach, the half acre Garden is densely planted with an unusual collection of both common and endangered native species.
Hours: Always open
Fees: Free

Ravine St. Gardens
Palatka, FL
(904)326-4001
Mail: PO Box 152, Palatka, FL 32178
Web: www.flazaleafest.com
🌺 The 25-acre is best known for its more than 100,000 azaleas representing 50 varieties that bloom from January through April. Other features include sub-tropical trees, native shrubs and flowers, formal gardens and natural settings of streams and ponds.
Hours: 9am-6pm daily
Fees: $3 per car; $1 if walking

Sarasota Jungle Gardens
3701 Bayshore Road
Sarasota, FL 34234
(941)355-5305
Web: www.sarasotajunglegardens.com
🌺 This site includes many acres of gardens and nature trails with trees, flowers and shrubs from all over the world.

Simpson Park Hammock
55 SW 17th Road
Miami, FL 33129
🌿 On 8.5 acres in downtown Miami, the site is the only remaining part of what was once a vast sub-tropical jungle. The conditions in the park parallel those of over one hundred years ago, with representative trees, plants and wildlife of South Florida.
Hours: 10am-5pm
Fees: Free

Sugar Mill Gardens
Old Sugar Mill Road
Port Orange, FL 32119
(904)767-1735
Location: Just south of Datona Beach
Web: www.ecotourism.org
🌿 Still a work-in-progress, the Gardens feature lilies, daylilies, azaleas, a bog trail, water garden, magnolia collection, Audubon trail, camellia collection, hollies, gingers, a xeriscape garden and the old sugar mill from which the site gets its name.
Hours: Dawn-dusk year round
Fees: Free; donations appreciated

University of Miami John C. Gifford Arboretum
San Amaro Drive & Robbia Avenue
Miami, FL
(305)284-5364
Mail: PO Box 249118, Coral Gables, FL 33124
Web: fig.cox.miami.edu/Arboretum/gifford.html
🌿 The Arboretum includes major tropical tree families with a good collection of trees native to southern Florida. Detailed labeling highlights some of the most interesting specimens

and there are trails for self-guided tours.
Fees: Free

University of South Florida Botanical Garden
Pine & Alumni Drives (SW corner of campus)
Tampa, FL
(813)974-2329
Mail: 4202 East Fowler, SCA 238, Tampa, FL 33620
Web: www.cas.usf.edu/envir_sci_policy/botanical/gardenfaq.html
🌿 The site includes a collection of fruit trees and palms from around the world, a bromeliad garden, herb garden, carnivorous plant bog, riparian wetland forest and a collection of rare begonias that may be seen by appointment.

Washington Oaks State Gardens
6400 North Oceanshore Blvd
Palm Coast, FL 32137-2415
(904)446-6780
Web: www.flausa.com
🌿 Located between the Atlantic Ocean and the Matanzas River, the 389-acre site features coastal scenery, a number of gardens and a citrus grove established by the New York family who wintered here up to the 1960s.

GEORGIA
See also Events for Georgia.

Atlanta Botanical Garden
1345 Piedmont Avenue NE
Atlanta, GA 30309
(404)876-5859
Web: www.atlantabotanicalgarden.org

🐚 Located on 30 acres in Piedmont Park, the Garden features the Fuqua Conservatory as its centerpiece with displays of more than 6,000 plant species from tropical and desert regions, home to birds and poison-arrow frogs from the South American rain forests. Outdoor highlights include the rose, perennial, herb, wildflower, vegetable and rock gardens, and a 5-acre upper woodland garden of camellias.

Atlanta History Center
130 West Paces Ferry Road NW
Atlanta, GA 30305
(404)814-4000
Web: www.atlantahistorycenter.com
🐚 The 33-acre Center displays the horticul-tural history of Atlanta and the natural suc-cession of native plants in Piedmont Georgia. It features a number of special gar-dens, ranging from a recently restored box-wood garden to quarry and farm gardens, plus woods trails and study stations.
Hours: 10am-5:30pm Mon-Sat, noon-5:30pm Sun
Fees: $10; $8 seniors & students; $5 children

Callaway Gardens
US Highway 27
Pine Mountain, GA
(800)225-5292
Location: 1 hour southwest of Atlanta
Mail: PO Box 2000, Pine Mountain, GA 31822
Web: www.callawaygardens.com
🐚 The Gardens comprise 14,000 acres of gardens, woodlands and lakes with indige-nous wildlife. Highlights include the newly constructed discover center with interactive

displays, a butterfly center with more than 1,000 butterflies year-round, a 40-acre azalea bowl in full bloom at the end of March, a 7.5-acre demonstration vegetable garden and a large herb garden.
Hours: 9am-5pm; extended hours in warmer months
Fees: $10; $5 children 6-12; children under 5 free; all fees plus tax

Elachee Nature Science Center
2125 Elachee Drive
Gainesville, GA 30504
(770)535-1976
Location: 50 miles from Atlanta
Web: www.elachee.net
🐚 The 1200-acre site features nature trails, a native plant garden, live animal displays and a museum, designed to educate the public about the environment and how to protect it for future generations.

Fernbank Museum of Natural History
767 Clifton Road NE
Atlanta, GA 30307-1221
(404)929-6300
Web: www.fernbank.edu
🐚 On the grounds of the Museum is the Robert L. Staton Rose Garden, one of only three sites in the U.S. for both AARS and ARS test roses. It is planted with approxi-mately 1,300 roses.
Hours: At all times
Fees: Free

Founders Memorial Garden
325 South Lumpkin Street
Athens, GA 30603
(706)542-8972
🐚 The site is a living memorial to the

founders of the Ladies' Garden Club of Athens, the first garden club in America. The 2.5-acre garden features a formal boxwood garden, courtyards, a retrace, a perennial garden and an arboretum.

Lockerly Arboretum
1534 Irwinton Road
Milledgeville, GA 31061
(912)452-2112
Location: 30 miles from Macon
Web: www.lockerlyarboretum.org
🌱 The 50-acre Arboretum is comprised of rolling topography typical of the Piedmont. The site is a horticultural laboratory rather than a showplace garden, with labeled trees and shrubs from all over the world.
Hours: Jun-Sep 8:30am-4:30pm Mon-Fri, Sat 10am-2pm; Oct-May 1-5pm
Fees: Free

Massee Lane Gardens
100 Massee Lane
Fort Valley, GA 31030
(912)967-2358
Location: 30 miles from Macon
Web: www.camellias-acs.com/MasseeLane/index.html
🌱 Home of the American Camellia Society, the site comprises 10 acres of towering pine trees which shade more than 2,000 camellias, in bloom from November through March. Other highlights include a greenhouse, Japanese garden, roses and many spring bloomers, including dogwoods, azaleas and bulbs.

Rock City Gardens
1400 Patten Road
Lookout Mountain, GA 30750
(706)820-2531
Location: less than 6 miles from Chattanooga, TN
Web: www.seerockcity.com
🌱 On the Tennessee border 1,700 feet above sea level, this 14-acre natural attraction features one of America's most unique sandstone formations where more than 700 species of native plants thrive. Highlights include spectacular chasms and crevices, home to a wide variety of lichens.
Hours: Open year round; Memorial Day-Labor Day 8:30am-8pm
Fees: $10.95; $5.95 children 3-12

State Botanical Garden of Georgia
2450 South Milledge Avenue
Athens, GA 30605
(706)542-1244
Web: www.uga.edu/botgarden/
🌱 Set in a preserve of over 300 acres, this young Garden has international, shade, rose, native flora, annual, perennial, dahlia, trial and herb gardens, as well as collections of rhododendrons, ground covers and native azaleas. There are five miles of nature trails.
Hours: Oct-Mar 8am-6pm; Apr-Sep 8am-8pm; Conservatory 9am-4:30pm Mon-Sat, 11:30am-4:30pm Sun
Fees: Free

Vines Botanical Gardens
3500 Oak Grove Road
Loganville, GA 30052
(770)466-7532
Web: www.vinesbotanicalgardens.com
🌱 The Gardens comprise 25 acres of developed gardens with a many different water features and antique statuary from Italy,

Yugoslavia and France. Highlights include Asian, white, rose colonnade and whimsical gardens. A 3.5-acre lake in the center of the Gardens is home to swans, geese and ducks.
Hours: 10am-5pm Tues-Sat; 11am-5pm Sat
Fees: $5; $4 seniors, children 5-12; children under 5 free

KENTUCKY
See also Events for Kentucky.

Bernheim Arboretum & Research Forest
Highway 245
Clermont, KY
(502)955-8512 or hotline (502)955-8822
Location: 25 miles south of Louisville
Mail: PO Box 130, Clermont, KY 40110
Web: www.bernheim.org
The site encompasses 16,000 acres of forest, landscaped areas, gardens and lakes, with 35 miles of hiking trails. Highlights of the Arboretum include collections of hollies, conifers, ornamental pears, dogwoods and beeches.

Broadmoor Garden & Conservatory
U.S. Highway 60
Irvington, KY
(270)547-4200
Location: 45 miles southwest of Louisville
Mail: PO Box 387, Irvington, KY 40146
Situated on 400 acres of a 2400-acre farm, Broadmoor features extensive water gardens with pools, fountains and waterfalls, a tropical plant conservatory, rose gardens, iris and lily gardens, a 2-mile nature-wildflower trail and a picnic area.

Hours: Apr-Oct 15 by appointment
Fees: $10

LOUISIANA
See also Events for Louisiana.

The Gardens of the American Rose Center
8877 Jefferson-Paige Road
Shreveport, LA
(318)938-5402
Mail: American Rose Society, PO Box 30,000, Shreveport, LA 71130-0030
Web: www.ars.org
The 118-acre site is America's largest park dedicated to the rose. More than 22,000 rosebushes, bubbling fountains and companion plants are displayed in over 65 individually landscaped gardens. Eight-passenger touring carts available for guided tours.
Hours: Apr-Oct 9am-5pm Mon-Fri, 9am-6pm Sat-Sun
Fees: $4; children under 12 free

Hermann-Grima Historic House
820 St. Louis Street
New Orleans, LA 70112
(504)525-5661
Web: www.gnofn.org/~hggh
In the heart of the French Quarter, the site offers a courtyard with original flagstone parterre beds filled with flowering plants documented to mid-19th century New Orleans.

Hodges Gardens & Wilderness
Highway 171 south of Many
Many, LA
(318)586-3523
Mail: PO Box 340, Florien, LA 71429

Web: www.hodgespark.com

🕯 The site is a combination of natural scenic areas and formal gardens, tucked in the rolling pine lands of west central Louisiana. Highlights include seasonal displays, a rose garden, greenhouses and views across a 225-acre lake to east Texas.

Jungle Gardens
Highway 329
Avery Island, LA
(318)369-6243
Location: near New Iberia
Mail: PO Box 126, Avery Island, LA 70513
🕯 Jungle Gardens was founded by Edward A. McIlhenny as a preserve for the endangered snowy egret. It is home to a large collection of camellias, azaleas, wildflowers and other plants from all over the world. Among the highlights are a marsh trail, live oaks, a sunken garden and a palm garden.

Longue Vue House & Gardens
7 Bamboo Road
New Orleans, LA 70124
(504)488-5488
Web: www.longuevue.com
🕯 The 8-acre Gardens surround a Greek Revival country house on the outskirts of New Orleans. Highlights include the Spanish water garden, an English country garden, a yellow garden, lily pond, orchid greenhouse and collections of camellias, magnolias and roses.

Louisiana State Arboretum
4213 Chicot Park Road
Ville Platte, LA
(318)363-6289
Mail: PO Box 494 Route 3, Ville Platte,

LA 70586

🕯 The Arboretum is a 300-acre living museum of trees, featuring plants native to Louisiana. There are 2.5 miles of nature trails which lead through mature beech and magnolia forests.
Hours: 9am-5pm
Fees: Free

New Orleans Botanical Garden
City Park, 1 Palm Drive
New Orleans, LA 70124
(504)483-9386
Web: www.neworleanscitypark.com/garden/
🕯 The Garden typifies the 1930s Art Deco movement in architecture and sculpture. Highlights include a water lily pond, parterre, formal rose garden, ancient live oaks, a butterfly walk and a collection of exotic tropical flora in the conservatory.
Hours: 10am-4:30pm Tues-Sun
Fees: $3; $1 children 5-12

Rip Van Winkle Gardens
5505 Rip Van Winkle Road
New Iberia, LA 70560
(800)375-3332 or (318)365-3332
Location: 20 miles from Lafayette
Web: www.ripvanwinkle.com
🕯 Highlights of this 25-acre site include a formal English garden, an Alhambra garden, magnolia garden, tropical glen, woodland garden, as well as good collections of camellias and Louisiana iris. Woodland paths connect the various gardens.

Rosedown Plantation & Gardens
12501 Highway 10
St. Francisville, LA 70775

(225)635-3332
Directions: Highway 10 & 61 North
One of the earliest of the 19th century historic gardens, these 28 acres have been continuously cultivated for 165 years. Former owners Daniel and Martha Turnbull were among the earliest to import camellias, azaleas and cryptomeria. A prime time to visit is early March through early April at the height of the blooming period.

Shadows-on-the-Teche

317 East Main Street
New Iberia, LA 70560
(337)369-6446
Location: 18 miles from Lafayette
Web: www.shadowsontheteche.org
The gardens of Shadows-on-the-Teche combine 19th and 20th century styles. Features include formal ornamental plantings and vistas, as well as secluded landscaped areas accessed by paths beneath the live oaks.
Hours: 9am-4:30pm; guided tours by reservation
Fees: $6; $3 children

Zemurray Gardens

23115 Zemurray Garden Drive
Loranger, LA 70446
(504)878-2284
Location: 15 mile northeast of Hammond on Hwy 40
The 150-acre Gardens feature a large collection of azaleas, camellias, dogwoods, wildflowers and Louisiana iris. The site includes a 2-mile graveled pathway surrounding a 20-acre lake which is open to the public for self-guided tours from March to mid-April.

Hours: 10am-6pm March-mid-April
Fees: $4; $3 seniors & children under 12

MISSISSIPPI

See also Events for Mississippi.

The Crosby Arboretum at MSU

370 Ridge Road
Picayune, MS 39466
(601)799-2311
Location: 50 miles from New Orleans
Web: www.msstate.edu/dept/crec/camain.html
Opened in the mid 1980s, this relatively new Arboretum specializes in plants of the local Pearl River Basin. Many species of trees, shrubs, wildflowers and grasses have been planted and plans are underway for expansion.

Gulfhaven Gardens

15429 CC Camp Road
Gulfport, MS 39503
(228)832-6424
Web: www.gulfhavengardens.com
The Gardens feature an American Hemerocallis Society display garden of 1,000 daylilies, as well as wildflowers, hummingbird and butterfly-attracting plants. It is landscaped with red maples, pines, birch trees and oaks. Peak daylily bloom is April and May.
Hours: Mar 15-May 30 9am-3pm Mon-Fri; also open by appointment
Fees: Free

Mynelle Gardens

4736 Clinton Blvd
Jackson, MS 39209
(601)960-1894

🌺 The 6-acre site dates from 1920 and includes thousands of azaleas, magnolias, gardenias, camellias, a rose garden and a Japanese-style area. It's known for daylily hybridizing.

Wister Gardens
500 Henry Road
Belzoni, MS 39038
(601)247-3025
🌺 The Gardens comprise 14 acres surrounding a colonial house. Features include 8,000 azaleas, rose gardens, fruit trees, an Italian fountain, gazebo, a lake and an excellent fall display of chrysanthemums, both outdoors and in greenhouses.
Hours: 8am-5pm
Fees: Free

NORTH CAROLINA
See also Events for North Carolina.

Biltmore Estate
Asheville, NC
(800)543-2961
Mail: 1 North Pack Square, Asheville, NC 28801
Web: www.biltmore.com
🌺 Biltmore is the 1895 French Renaissance residence of George Washington Vanderbilt. The grounds and gardens were designed by Frederick Law Olmsted and feature a newly refurbished conservatory.

The Botanical Gardens at Asheville
151 W.T. Weaver Boulevard
Asheville, NC 28804
(828)252-5190

🌺 The Garden specializes in native plants of the South Appalachian region and has collections of rhododendrons, azaleas and wildflowers.
Hours: 9:30am-4:30pm
Fees: Free

Cape Fear Botanical Garden
536 North Eastern Blvd
Fayetteville, NC
(910)486-0221
Mail: PO Box 53485, Fayetteville, NC 28305
Web: www.capefearbg.org
🌺 Located on 85 acres, the Garden includes a large urban forest, a natural amphitheater, an 1880s homestead with outbuildings, a heritage garden, formal gardens and trails leading to bluffs overlooking Cross Creek and the Cape Fear River.
Hours: 10am-5pm; noon-5pm Sun except mid Dec-mid Feb
Fees: $3

Daniel Boone Native Gardens
Horn in the West Drive
Boone, NC
(828)264-6390
Location: 75 miles from Winston-Salem
Mail: 295 Grover Johnson Raod, Vilas, NC 28692
🌺 The 10-acre Gardens feature a collection of native North Carolina plants in an informal landscape, with pools, sunken garden, rock garden and meadows. They are supported and maintained by the Garden Club of North Carolina, Inc.
Hours: May-Oct 9am-6pm
Fees: $2

Daniel Stowe Botanical Garden
6500 South New Hope Road
Belmont, NC 28012
(704)825-4490
Location: West of Charlotte
Web: www.dsbg.org
Opened in 1999, the new 110-acre facility features four themed gardens, a dozen fountains, a visitor's pavilion and a half-mile woodland trail. The new gardens are part of a 450-acre master plan that will take several decades.
Hours: 9am-6pm summer; 9am-5pm winter
Fees: Weekdays $6, $3 children 6-12; weekends & holidays $8, $4 children 6-12; Tuesdays mornings free to individuals

Elizabethan Gardens
Highway 64/264
Roanoke Island, NC
(252)473-3234
Mail: 1411 Highway 64/264, Manteo, NC 27954
Web: www.outerbanks.com/elizabethangardens/info.htm
On the site of the first English colony in the New World, the Gardens feature a sunken garden, Shakespeare's herb garden, woodland garden and wildlife garden. Seasonal highlights include azaleas, dogwoods, gardenias, roses and magnolias.

Greenfield Gardens
Wilmington, NC
(910)341-7883
Mail: Department of Parks, PO Box 1810, Wilmington, NC 28402
The Gardens are located in a city park on five miles of lake front and include display gardens, fragrance garden and azaleas.

J.C. Raulston Arboretum at NCSU
4301 Beryl Road
Raleigh, NC 27606
(919)515-3132
Mail: Department of Horticultural Science, Box 7609, NC State University, Raleigh, NC 27695-6709
Web: arb.ncsu.edu
The Arboretum features 8 acres of special gardens designed to evaluate and promote well-adapted plants for home landscaping. Highlights include a white garden, a Japanese garden and a 450-foot perennial border.
Fees: Free

Montrose Gardens
320 St. Marys Road
Hillsborough, NC
(919)732-7787
Mail: PO Box 957, Hillsborough, NC 27278
Montrose is a 20-acre complex of gardens begun in the mid 1800s by Governor William Alexander Graham and now privately owned. Highlights include a rock garden, scree garden, numerous sunny gardens and several extensive woodland gardens.
Hours: Guided tours by appointment 10am Tues, Thurs, Sat
Fees: $6

North Carolina Arboretum
100 Frederick Law Olmstead Way
Asheville, NC 28806
(828)665-2492
Web: www.ncarboretum.org
Located on the edge of Pisgah National Forest, this site comprises 426 acres of wooded areas, 80 acres of which have been

developed with formal gardens and land-scaped areas. It includes a state-of-the-art greenhouse complex and a loop trail.

North Carolina Botanical Garden
University of North Carolina, Laurel Hill Road
Chapel Hill, NC
(919)962-0522
Mail: CB Box 3375, Totten Center, UNC, Chapel Hill, NC 27599
Web: www.unc.edu/depts/ncbg
🌿 The display gardens feature wildflowers, ferns, aquatics, carnivorous and poisonous plants as well as an extensive herb garden. The arboretum contains a woodland of mature pines, some virgin forest, a collection of indigenous trees, shrubs and flowers of the southeast. There are two miles of nature trails.
Hours: Dawn-dusk
Fees: Free

Orton Plantation Gardens
9149 Orton Road, SE
Winnabow, NC 28479
(910)371-6851
Location: 18 miles south of Wilmington
🌿 The site features formal and informal gardens surrounding an antebellum house. Special highlights include impressive oaks and other native trees, expansive lawns and scenic vistas over the old rice fields and Cape Fear River. Spring is the best time to visit when camellias, azaleas, flowering trees and ornamentals are in bloom.
Hours: Mar-Aug 8am-6pm; Sep-Nov 10am-5pm
Fees: $8; $7 seniors

Raleigh Municipal Rose Garden
301 Pogue Street
Raleigh, NC
(919)890-3285
Mail: Raleigh Parks & Recreation Department, 4225 Daly Road, Raleigh, NC 27604
🌿 The 3-acre Garden is a display garden for the AARS and features a large variety of roses from old roses to hybrid teas.

Reynolda Gardens of Wake Forest University
100 Reynolda Village
Winston-Salem, NC 27106
(336)758-5593
Web: www.wfu.edu/gardens/
🌿 This 129-acre site was originally part of the estate of Richard Joshua Reynolds. Highlights include an early Lord and Burnham greenhouse, formal gardens designed by Thomas Sears, a rose garden, border gardens and mixed flower and vegetable garden.
Hours: Dawn-dusk; Greenhouse 10am-4pm Mon-Fri, closed Sat, Sun
Fees: Free

Sarah P. Duke Gardens
West Campus of Duke University, adjacent to the Medical Center
Durham, NC
(919)684-3698
Mail: PO Box 90341, Durham, NC 27708
Web: www.hr.duke.edu/dukegardens/
🌿 The Gardens comprise 55 acres of landscaped and woodland gardens with five miles of allées, walks and pathways through formal and informal gardens. Special features include terraces designed by Ellen

Biddle Shipman, a native plant garden and an Asiatic arboretum.
Hours: 8am-dusk
Fees: Free

Tryon Palace Historic Sites & Gardens
610 Pollock Street
New Bern, NC
(800) 767-1560
Mail: PO Box 1007, New Bern, NC 28563
Web: www.tryonpalace.org
The Gardens of Tryon Palace reflect a variety of styles, from the simple gardens of Colonial times to the complex landscaping of the high Victorian era. Features include the grand entrance allée, a kitchen garden, 18th century ornamental plantings and a wilderness garden.
Hours: Memorial Day-Labor Day 7am-7pm Mon-Sat, 1-7pm Sun; rest of year 9am-5pm Mon-Sat, 1-5pm Sun
Fees: Fee charged

UNC Charlotte Botanical Gardens
Mary Alexander Road & Craver Road
Charlotte, NC 28223
(704)687-4055
Mail: Biology Department, UNCC, 9201 University City Blvd, Charlotte, NC 28223
Web: www.bioweb.uncc.edu/gardens/
There are several outstanding special collections in this 9-acre Garden, including hardy ornamentals, rhododendron hybrids and Carolina natives. Other highlights include collections of orchids, succulents and carnivorous plants in the greenhouse.
Hours: Gardens daylight hours every day; Greenhouse 10am-3pm Mon-Sat
Fees: Free

Wilkes Community College Gardens
Wilkesboro, NC
(336)838-6100
Location: 55 miles from Winston-Salem
Mail: PO Box 120, Wilkesboro, NC 28697
Web: www.wilkes.cc.nc.us
On a 140-acre site, the Gardens include a sensory garden, rose garden, Japanese garden, native gardens and a one-mile walking trail, plus an extensive collection of evergreens.
Hours: Dawn-dusk
Fees: Free

Wilson Rose Garden
1800 Herring Avenue
Wilson, NC
(800)497-7398
Mail: PO Box 10, Wilson, NC 27894
Web: www.wilson-nc.com/wct_rosegarden.html
The 2-acre Garden features more than 1,000 roses representing 145 varieties, including All-America Rose Selections. Another highlight is original sculpture and wrought iron work, including the 10' Georgia marble sculpture by internationally known sculptor Horace Farlowe. A pecan grove picnic area adjoins the Garden.
Hours: Dawn-dark
Fees: Free

Wing Haven Gardens & Bird Sanctuary
248 Ridgewood Avenue
Charlotte, NC 28209
(704)331-0664
Situated in the heart of a residential neighborhood not far from uptown Charlotte, this unique 4-acre Sanctuary attracts birds with carefully-designed water

elements and plantings that provide food, cover and nesting sites. It includes formal gardens and wooded areas with ferns and wildflowers.
Hours: Gardens 2-5pm Sun, 3-5pm Tues, 10am-noon Wed; tours by appointment
Fees: Free

PUERTO RICO

Jardin Botanico
Rio Piedras, University of Puerto Rico
San Juan, PR
(787)767-1710
Directions: South of Hwy 1 & Rte 84 intersection
Mail: University of Puerto Rico, Box 364984, San Juan, PR 00936
🏛 A highlight of the site is the Monet garden, based on the artist's gardens at Giverny and adapted to this tropical milieu. Other features include heliconia, orchid and aquatic gardens, a palmtum, herbarium and bamboo chapel.
Hours: 9am-4pm
Fees: Free

SOUTH CAROLINA

See also Events for South Carolina.

Brookgreen Gardens
1931 Brookgreen Gardens Drive, Highway 17S
Murrels Inlet, SC
(843)237-4218
Location: 20 miles south of Myrtle Beach
Mail: PO Box 3368, Pawley's Island,

SC 29585
Web: www.brookgreen.org
🏛 Set on 300 acres in the midst of a 9,100-acre preserve stretching from the Atlantic Ocean to the historic rice fields of the Waccamaw River, Brookgreen Gardens is the work of sculptor Anna Hyatt Huntington and her husband. An allée of 200-year old live oaks leads to a series of informal, connecting gardens which provide a background for the sculpture.

Cypress Gardens
3030 Cypress Gardens Road
Moncks Corner, SC 29461
(843)553-0515
Location: Near Charleston
🏛 Originally part of one of the Cooper River's most important rice plantations, the 163-acre Gardens feature spring displays of azaleas, dogwoods and wisteria as well as a small working rice field which is planted and harvested using centuries-old methods. It can be accessed by nature trails or in a flat-bottomed boat.

Edisto Memorial Gardens
Highway 301 South
Orangeburg, SC
(803)534-6376
Mail: PO Box 863, Orangeburg, SC 29115
🏛 The Gardens encompass over 150 acres of landscaped areas and a wetlands park traversed by a boardwalk. Highlights include butterfly and sensory gardens, as well as an All-America Rose Selections test garden, with over 50 beds of roses ranging from miniatures to grandifloras and climbers.
Hours: Dawn-dusk
Fees: Free

Kalmia Gardens of Coker College
1624 West Carolina Avenue
Hartsville, SC 29550
(843)383-8145
Web: www.coker.edu/kalmia/
🌿 Located on the bluffs of Black Creek, the Gardens comprise 30 acres on the site of the early 19th century plantation of Captain Thomas E. Hart. Highlights include an AHS Daylily Display Garden, a black water swamp, laurel thickets, a collection of ornamentals and uplands of pine, oak and holly.
Hours: Dawn-dusk
Fees: Free

Magnolia Plantation & Gardens
3550 Ashley River Road
Charleston, SC 29414
(843)571-1266
Web: www.magnoliaplantation.com
🌿 Dating from 1676, this informal British-style estate is still owned by the Drayton heirs and is America's oldest continually-planted garden. Features include one of the largest collections of azaleas and camellias in the country, a maze, Barbados tropical garden, Biblical garden, herb garden, topiary garden and Audubon swamp garden.

Middleton Place Gardens
4300 Ashley River Road
Charleston, SC 29414
(843)556-6020
Location: 14 miles northwest of Charleston
Web: www.middletonplace.org
🌿 Established in 1741 by Henry Middleton, President of the First Continental Congress, the 65-acre Gardens overlooking the Ashley River reflect the grand classic style and principles of Le Notre, with attention to woods,

water, vistas, focal points and surprises. Highlights include camellias, azaleas, kalmia, magnolias, crape myrtle and roses.
Hours: 9am-5pm
Fees: $15; $7 children 6-12; house tour additional $8 all ages

Riverbanks Zoo & Botanical Gardens
500 Wildlife Parkway
Columbia, SC
(803)779-8717
Mail: PO Box 1060, Columbia, SC 29202
Web: www.riverbanks.org
🌿 Located on the west bank of the Saluda River across from Riverbanks Zoo, the 70-acre site features a football field-size walled garden with a 300 foot long canal, cascades and fountains, surrounded by an eight-foot brick wall. Other highlights include an old rose garden and nature trails with views over the river.
Hours: 9am-4pm; til 5pm summer weekends & holidays
Fees: $6.25; $3.75 children 3-12

Singing Oaks Garden
1019 Abell Road
Blythewood, SC 29016
(803)786-1351
Location: Near Columbia
🌿 A private garden, the site is an accredited AHS Display Garden with over 2,000 different daylily cultivars and many companion trees, shrubs and perennials.
Hours: May 15-July 15, or by appointment
Fees: Free

The South Carolina Botanical Garden
102 Garden Trail, Clemson University
Clemson, SC 29634

(864)656-3405
Location: 30 miles from Greenville
Web: virtual.clemson.edu/scbg/
🔱 Highlights of this 270-acre site are the many niche gardens, including a camellia garden, wildlife habitat, wildflower meadow, conifer garden, xeriscape garden and woodland wildflower garden, all accessed by a nature trail.
Hours: Dawn to dusk
Fees: Free

Swan Lake Iris Gardens
822 West Liberty Street
Sumter, SC
(800)688-4748
Mail: PO Box 1449, Sumter, SC 29151
Web: www.uscsumter.edu/~sumter/
iris.html
🔱 This 160-acre park creates a natural setting for azaleas, camellias and one of the largest iris gardens in the country.
Hours: 8am-dusk
Fees: Free

TENNESSEE
See also Events for Tennessee.

Cheekwood Botanical Garden
1200 Forrest Park Drive
Nashville, TN 37205
(615)356-8000
Web: www.cheekwood.org
🔱 The 55-acre Garden features a number of gardens, including wildflower, herb study, color, trial and Japanese gardens, as well as a newly renovated water garden. A new mile-long sculpture trail winds through

woods and is lined with contemporary works by national and international artists.

Dixon Gallery & Gardens
4339 Park Avenue
Memphis, TN 38117
(901)761-5250
Web: www.dixon.org
🔱 Created out of 17 acres of native Tennessee woodland, the Gardens are landscaped in the English park style with open vistas and formal gardens. Highlights includes a woodland garden, cutting garden, a camellia conservatory and a greenhouse.

The Hermitage: Home of President Andrew Jackson
4580 Rachel's Lane
Hermitage, TN 37076
(615)889-2941
Location: 12 miles from Nashville
Web: www.thehermitage.com
🔱 Designed In 1819 by English gardener William Frost for Andrew Jackson, the garden was subsequently developed by the owner's wife, Rachel Jackson, with ornamental plantings. Laid out as a near perfect one-acre square, the garden features the same old-fashioned flowers and shrubs that bloomed in it more than 170 years ago.

Memphis Botanic Garden
750 Cherry Road
Memphis, TN 38117
(901)685-1566
Web: www.memphisbotanicgarden.com
🔱 The 96-acre Garden contains many special areas, including Japanese, iris, magno-

lia, rose, daffodil, dahlia and wildflower gardens. Highlights include excellent specimens of Japanese cherry trees, holly, crabapples and native shrubs. The conservatory contains collections of crotons, orchids and bromeliads.

Reflection Riding Arboretum & Botanical Garden
400 Garden Road
Chattanooga, TN 37419
(423)821-9582
Web: virtual.chattanooga.net/rriding
🌺 Reflection Riding is a 300-acre botanical garden, home to a variety of trees, shrubs and flowers. Visitors can walk, bike or drive the three mile loop or hike for miles up Lookout Mountain or along Lookout Creek.

University of Tennessee Arboretum
901 Kerr Hollow Road
Oak Ridge, TN 37830
(423)483-3571
🌺 The 260-acre Arboretum features woody plants, dogwoods, conifers, viburnums, hollies, landscape plants and native species.

University of Tennessee Gardens
UT Agriculture Campus
Knoxville, TN
(865)974-7324
Mail: University of Tennessee Institute of Agriculture, PO Box 1071, Knoxville, TN 37901
Web: web.utk.edu/~hort/
🌺 The 5-acre Gardens feature over 500 perennials, 600 annuals, many herbs and hundreds of trees, on view from a winding brick path.

VIRGIN ISLANDS
See also Events for Virgin Islands.

St. George Village Botanical Garden
127 Estate St. George
Frederiksted, VI 00840
(340)692-2874
🌺 Built on the site of an 18th century sugar cane plantation, the 17-acre Garden features over 1,600 native and exotic varieties against the backdrop of restored and stabilized plantation buildings. Its collections include exotic rain forest, cactus and succulent gardens, orchid collections and the ethnobotanical collection called Heritage Gardens.

VIRGINIA
See also Events for Virginia.

Agecroft Hall
4305 Sulgrave Road
Richmond, VA 23221
(804)353-4241
Web: www.agecrofthall.com
🌺 Overlooking the James River, the 23-acre site includes Tudor and Stuart period style gardens and a 15th century English manor house, dismantled and moved to this site in the 20th century.

American Horticultural Society
7931 East Boulevard Drive
Alexandria, VA 22308
(800)777-7931
Web: www.ahs.org
🌺 AHS national headquarters is located at the 25-acre River Farm, once owned by

George Washington. Maps are available at the visitor center for self-guided tours of the lawns, gardens, meadows and woods on the banks of the Potomac River.

The Arboretum at James Madison University
Harrisonburg, VA
(540)568-3194
Mail: MSC 6901, Harrisonburg, VA 22807
Web: www.jmu.edu/external/arb/
🏵 The Arboretum consists of 125 acres of native oak and hickory forest with miles of trails winding through the diverse habitats. Highlights include one of Virginia's largest wildflower gardens, pond and bog gardens, a rhododendron collection and fern, herb and rock gardens.

Ashlawn Highland, Home of James Monroe
1000 James Monroe Parkway
Charlottesville, VA 22902
(804)293-9539
Web: www.monticello.avenue.org/ashlawn/
🏵 Originally the home of James Monroe, the estate and gardens have been restored to their original elegance. The site includes an old boxwood garden, an herb garden and a kitchen garden.

Colonial Williamsburg
Williamsburg, VA
(800)603-0948
Mail: Colonial Williamsburg Foundation, PO Box 1776, Williamsburg, VA 23187-1776
Web: www.history.org
🏵 There are 90 acres of residential gardens within the restoration, ranging from small kitchen gardens with herbs, vegetables and espaliered fruit trees to large geometric gardens featuring boxwood parterres, topiaries and heirloom flowers.

George Washington's Mount Vernon
South end of GW Memorial Parkway
Mount Vernon, VA
(703)780-2000
Mail: PO Box 110, Mount Vernon, VA 22121
Web: www.mountvernon.org
🏵 The gardens on the estate have been restored to reflect Washington's landscaping designs. Highlights include the upper "pleasure" garden, the lower "kitchen" garden planted with vegetables, herbs and fruit, and orchard and nursery used by Washington to experiment with new seeds.

Glen Burnie Historic House & Gardens
530 Amherst Street
Winchester, VA 22601
(540)662-1473
🏵 The site features 25 acres of formal gardens in a series of garden rooms. Spaces range from a small herb garden to a grand allée of flowering crabapple trees. Other highlights include a Chinese garden, formal vegetable garden, perennial cutting garden, rose gardens and water gardens.

Green Spring Gardens
4603 Green Springs Road
Alexandria, VA 22312
(703)642-5173
Web: www.greenspring.org
🏵 The 27-acre Gardens feature a variety of demonstration gardens that include the area's largest rock garden, extensive mixed borders, herb and vegetable gardens on a

domestic scale. The site includes an 18th century manor house and horticulture center.

Gunston Hall Plantation
10709 Gunston Road
Mason Neck, VA 22079
(703)550-9220
Location: 20 miles from Washington, DC
Web: www.GunstonHall.org
🕭 Gunston Hall was built by George Mason, framer of the United States Constitution and author of the Virginia Declaration of Rights. The house is surrounded by 550 acres featuring formal gardens that are currently in process of restoration and scheduled for completion in 2001.

Historic Kenmore
1201 Washington Avenue
Fredericksburg, VA 22401
(540)373-3381
Location: 55 miles from Washington, DC
Web: www.kenmore.org
🕭 Located on the grounds of Kenmore mansion, home of Fielding Lewis and his wife, the sister of George Washington, the 3-acre garden has been restored in the style of the period. Highlights include a formal parterre, cutting garden, kitchen yard garden, and a wilderness walk.

Lewis Ginter Botanical Garden
1800 Lakeside Avenue
Richmond, VA 23228
(804)262-9887
Web: www.lewisginter.org
🕭 The 25-acre site contains one of the largest and most diverse perennial gardens on the east coast. Other highlights include an elegant Victorian-style garden restored

by The Garden Club of Virginia, an Asian garden, a children's garden and a wetland environment with an excellent display of pitcher plants, water iris and lotus.

Mary Washington House & Garden
1200 Charles Street
Fredericksburg, VA 22401
(540)373-1569
Mail: Association for the Preservation of Virginia Antiquities, 1200 Charles Street, Fredericksburg, VA 22401
Web: www.fredericksburgva.com
🕭 Restored to reflect Mary Washington's original planting, the 3/4-acre Garden features a vegetable garden, an English-style flower garden, the original boxwoods and an authentic period sundial.

Maymont
2201 Shields Lake Drive
Richmond, VA
(804)358-7166
Mail: Maymont Foundation, 1700 Hampton Street, Richmond, VA 23220
Web: www.maymont.org
🕭 Formerly the estate of Major James H. Dooley, Maymont is an intact example of the elaborate showplaces fashionable among Gilded Age millionaires. It includes the opulent 1893 Maymont House and a 100-acre estate, with a Japanese garden, grotto, arboretum and Italian garden designed by Noland and Baskerville.

Norfolk Botanical Garden
6700 Azalea Garden Road
Norfolk, VA 23518
(757)441-5830
Web: www.virginiagarden.org

🌷 The Garden features one of the largest collections of azaleas, camellias and roses on the east coast. Its 155 acres include more than 25 theme gardens and a climate-controlled Tropical Pavilion. Boat and train tours are available.

Oatlands Plantation
20850 Oatlands Plantation Lane
Leesburg, VA 20175
(703)777-3174 or (800)752-3174
Web: www.oatlands.org
🌷 The estate includes formal gardens, terraced gardens with a 150-year old boxwood, gazebo, reflecting pool, specimen oaks planted by the original owner, plus magnolias, a boxwood allée, a bowling green and many species of trees and flowering shrubs. This Federal style mansion of 1800 has been completely restored.

The Old Rose Garden at Ben Lomond Manor House
10311 Sudley Manor Drive
Manassas, VA
(703)369-6925 or (703)368-8784
Location: Interstate 66, 40 minutes west of DC
Mail: Ben Lomond Community Center, 10501 Copeland Drive, Manassas, VA 20109
Web: www.geocities.com/~oldrosegarden/
🌷 The Garden features an antique rose collection dating from the 1800s representing 160 varieties.

Sherwood Forest Plantation
John Tyler Highway
Charles City, VA
(804)829-5377

🌷 Once home of John Tyler, the 10th President, this 19th century house is surrounded by its original outbuildings and 25 acres of terraced gardens and lawns. Considered to be one of the most complete plantation yards left in America, the site got its name from Tyler's reputation as a political outlaw.

State Arboretum of Virginia
400 Blandy Farm Lane
Boyce, VA 22620
(540)837-1758
Location: 9 miles east of Winchester
Web: www.virginia.edu/~blandy/home.html
🌷 The Arboretum features the largest collection of boxwood in North America and an extensive collection of more than half the world's pine species. Other features include a Virginia native plant trail, herb garden, daylilies and azaleas. A three mile loop drive winds through a grove of 350 ginkgo trees.

Stratford Hall Plantation
Route 214
Stratford, VA
(804)493-8038 or (804)493-8371
weekends & holidays
Mail: Robert E. Lee Memorial Association, Stratford Hall, Stratford, VA 22558
Web: www.stratfordhall.org
🌷 The birthplace of Robert E. Lee, this plantation is operated as it would have been in the mid-19th century. In addition to cultivated fields, woodlands and meadows, there are formal gardens with boxwood hedges, a rose garden, herb and kitchen gardens.

Tuckahoe Plantation
12601 River Road
Richmond, VA 23233
(804)784-6774
Location: 7 miles west of Richmond
🌿 At one point the boyhood home of Thomas Jefferson, this 1712 estate reflects early 18th century design. Features include a vegetable garden with screening boxwoods, a formal garden, a kitchen garden of herbs and perennials, as well as early outbuildings which border a plantation "street."

Woodlawn Plantation
9000 Richmond Highway
Alexandria, VA 22309
(703)780-4000
🌿 Originally a wedding gift for George Washington's foster daughter, the site includes 20 acres of gardens which have been carefully restored. Among the highlights are parterre gardens of old fashioned roses which peak in late May, views overlooking the Potomac and nature trails.

Woodrow Wilson Birthplace & Gardens
18-24 North Coalter Street
Staunton, VA
(540)885-0897
Location: 10 miles from Waynesboro
Mail: PO Box 24, Staunton, VA 24402
Web: www.woodrowwilson.org
🌿 The 1-acre Gardens were restored in the early 1930s by Charles F. Gillette. Highlights include boxwoods and terraced gardens.

WEST VIRGINIA
See also Events for West Virginia.

Core Arboretum
Monongahela Blvd, WVU Evansdale Campus
Morgantown, WV
(304)293-5201
Mail: WVU Department of Biology, PO Box 6057, Morgantown, WV 26506
🌿 The 75-acre Arboretum along the Monongahela River comprise a number of natural habitats ranging from open fields to wooded hillside and bottom land. Highlights include special collections of viburnums, heaths, ferns, herbs and wildflowers.

Sunshine Farm & Gardens
Route 5GT
Renick, WV 24966
(304)497-2208
Web: www.sunfarm.com
🌿 The 60-acre site is the garden, arboretum, nursery and home of avid plant collector, Barry Glick. It features more than 10,000 different plant varieties, 68,000 hellebores, in bloom from February through May, and over 500 different peony cultivars, in bloom from May to June.
Hours: By appointment
Fees: Free

SELECTED EVENTS FOR THE SOUTHEAST

Selections for 2001 include the South's greatest shows, like the Virginia Flower & Garden Show in Virginia Beach, the Southeastern Flower Show in Atlanta, the Southern Spring Show in Charlotte, the Maymont Flower and Garden Show in Richmond, and the Antiques & Garden Show in Nashville, where this year royalty will be speaking.

There are marvelous festivals in the Southeast, such as the Iris Festival in Sumter, the Dogwood Festivals in Atlanta and Knoxville, the Royal Poinciana Festival in Miami and the Azalea Festival in Palatka, Florida.

There are great open days programs, like the one sponsored by Garden Conservancy (see listing below), the statewide Historic Garden Week in Virginia, Charleston's Festival of Houses and Gardens, and Savannah's Tour of Homes and Gardens.

Throughout the region there are wonderful locally sponsored tours, festivals, shows and sales. Over 250 of the best are listed below, including 100 that appear for the first time in this edition.

REGIONWIDE

March - October
🌿 **The Garden Conservancy's Open Days Program**★★★★
The Garden Conservancy's Open Days Program is now in its seventh season. Through this program over 400 private gardens in 26 states were open to the public in 2000. In 2001, there will be Open Days in the following southeast states: Florida, Louisiana, Tennessee and Virginia. An Open Days Directory, published each year in the spring, provides garden descriptions, open dates and times, travel directions and a list of other public gardens in the area. It also includes a coupon for one free garden visit. Proceeds from admission benefit the Garden Conservancy's preservation pro-grams and are often shared with a local charity or not-for-profit organization of the garden host's choice. To receive information about the 2001 Open Days Program, other Conservancy programs or membership, contact the Conservancy.
The Garden Conservancy, PO Box 219, Cold Spring, NY 10516
Web: www.gardenconservancy.org
(888)842-2442 or (845)265-5384

ALABAMA
Birmingham

March 8-11
🌿 **Birmingham Home & Garden Show**
A large regional show featuring a variety of show gardens, informative seminars and an

25

extensive display of products and services for home and garden. Annual event, now in its 27th year.

Hours: 11am-9pm Thurs-Sat; 11am-6pm Sun

Fee: $7

Birmingham-Jefferson Convention Complex, 1 Civic Center Plaza, Birmingham, AL

Contact: **Exposition Enterprises, Inc.**, PO Box 430, Pinson, AL 35126

E-mail: expoei@wwisp.com

(800)226-3976 or (205)680-0234

April 6-7

🌱 **Spring Fiesta Plant Sale**

A huge sale of plant material including annuals, bonsai, daylilies, ferns, herbs, hostas, iris, native plants, perennials, rhododendron, roses, orchids, exotic vegetables, tropical plants, books and gardening accessories. Held under a big tent in the Gardens. Annual event.

Hours: 9am-5pm Fri; 9am-3pm Sat

Fee: Free

Birmingham Botanical Gardens, 2612 Lane Park Road, Birmingham, AL 35223

Web: www.bbgardens.org

(205)414-3900

September 21-23

🌱 **Birmingham Fall Home Show**

A large regional show featuring a variety of show gardens, informative seminars and an extensive display of products and services for home and garden. Annual event, now in its 18th year.

Hours: 11am-9pm Fri ; 11am-9pm Sat; 11am-6pm Sun

Birmingham-Jefferson Convention Complex, 1 Civic Center Plaza, Birmingham, AL

Contact: **Exposition Enterprises, Inc.** *See earlier listing in this section.*

E-mail: expoei@wwisp.com

(800)226-3976 or (205)680-0234

Dothan

May 5-6

🌱 **Spring Garden Tour**

A tour of twelve private gardens in the Wiregrass region with docents, refreshments and local musicians in each garden. A sale of plants, seeds and garden statuary at the Gardens on tour days. Annual event.

Hours: 10am-5pm Sat; 1-5pm Sun

Fee: $12; covers both days

Dothan Area Botanical Gardens, 5130 Headland Avenue, Dothan, AL 36303

Web: www.dabg.com

(334)793-3224

Huntsville

March 31 - April 29

🌱 **Festival of Flowers**

A festival to celebrate spring in the Garden, when the poppies, tulips, pansies, azaleas dogwoods and wildflowers reach peak bloom. Tours of the dogwood and wildflower trails, an indoor floral display in the new exhibit hall and many other activities. Call for schedule. Annual event.

The Huntsville-Madison County Botanical Garden, 4747 Bob Wallace Avenue, Huntsville, AL 35805

Web: www.hsvbg.org

(256)830-4447

Remember that schedules do change.

April 19-22
🌺 **Spring Plant Sale**
A huge sale of over 100,000 plants, includ-
ing heirloom and unusual plants, herbs,
wildflowers, vegetables, annuals, perenni-
als, shrubs and shrub trees, plus a garden
boutique. Held under tents on the Garden
grounds. Sponsored by The Garden Guild.
Annual event.
Hours: 9am-5pm
**The Huntsville-Madison County Botanical
Garden** *See earlier listing in this section.*
Web: www.hsvbg.org
(256)830-4447

May 5 - September 30
🌺 **Butterflies in the Tessmann Butterfly
House**
More than thirty species of North American
butterflies flying free inside a landscaped
enclosure. On view, butterflies in egg, cater-
pillar, chrysalis and adult stages. Special
display of red eared slider turtles in natural
habitat.
Hours: 8am-6:30pm Mon-Sat;
1-6:30pm Sun
Fee: Regular admission
**The Huntsville-Madison County Botanical
Garden** *See earlier listing in this section.*
Web: www.hsvbg.org
(256)830-4447

May 10
🌺 **Southern Living Gardening School**
An educational program presented by
Southern Living magazine. Lunch included.
Annual event.
Fee: Fee charged
The Huntsville-Madison County Botanical

Garden *See earlier listing in this section.*
Web: www.hsvbg.org
(256)830-4447

June 1-30
🌺 **Daylily & Fern Festivals**
Peak bloom of 600 varieties of daylilies and
a fern sale on the third weekend.
Annual event.
Hours: 8am-6:30 pm
Fee: Regular admission
**The Huntsville-Madison County Botanical
Garden** *See earlier listing in this section.*
Web: www.hsvbg.org
(256)830-4447

September - October
🌺 **Fall Family Festival**
Recommended for families. Special activi-
ties every weekend, including music in the
Garden, hay rides, a sorghum maze, scav-
enger hunts. Saturday morning garden
walks. Annual event.
Hours: 10am-5pm Sat-Sun
Fee: Regular admission
**The Huntsville-Madison County Botanical
Garden** *See earlier listing in this section.*
Web: www.hsvbg.org
(256)830-4447

November 22 - January 1, 2002
🌺 **Galaxy of Lights**
Recommended for families. A drive-through
light show billed as the Tennessee Valley's
largest and most spectacular. More than
150 illuminated creations on themes ranging from nursery rhymes to Jurassic Park.
"Jingle Bell Walk" open two nights with
Santa and vendors. Annual event.

Be sure to check with the sponsor in advance.

Hours: 5:30-9pm
Fee: $10 per car; $3 tour bus; Jingle Bell
Walk $5 adult & $2 children
**The Huntsville-Madison County Botanical
Garden** *See earlier listing in this section.*
Web: www.hsvbg.org
(256)830-4447

Mobile

March 2-4
🌿 Gulf Coast Home & Garden Show
A large regional show featuring a variety of
show gardens, seminars and an extensive
home and garden exhibit area. Held in a
beautiful facility right on the water with ter-
races overlooking the Mobile River.
Hours: 11am-9pm Fri-Sat; 11am-6pm Sun
Fee: $6
Mobile Convention Center, One South
Water Street, Mobile, AL
Contact: **Exposition Enterprises, Inc.**, PO
Box 430, Pinson, AL 35126
E-mail: expoei@wwisp.com
(800)226-3976 or (205)680-0234

March 22-25
🌿 Festival of Flowers
An outdoor show of life-size specially-
designed landscaped gardens by top
designers and hobbyists, floral displays,
plus plants, landscaping supplies and garden products for sale. Held when the azaleas of this 300 year-old city are in full
bloom. Annual event, now in its 8th year.
Hours: 9am-5pm Thurs-Sat; 11am-5pm
Sun
Fee: $6.50 in advance; $8.50 at gate; $2
children 7-12 at gate

Spring Hill College Campus, Dauphin
Street, 1/2 mile west of I-65, Mobile, AL
Contact: **Providence Hospital Foundation**,
PO Box 850429, Mobile, AL 36685
Web: www.FestivalofFlowers.com
(334)639-2050

May 11-13
🌿 Gallery of Gardens Tour
A self-guided tour of six of Mobile's most
interesting gardens in the Lincoln Park area.
Another tour in late September targets a dif-
ferent area. Annual event.
Mobile Botanical Gardens, PO Box 8382,
Mobile, AL 36689
(334)342-0555

Thanksgiving - December
🌿 Magic Christmas in Lights
Recommended for families. Millions of
lights and seasonal displays throughout the
grounds and home. Annual event.
Bellingrath Gardens & Home, 12401
Bellingrath Gardens Road, Theodore,
AL 36582
Web: www.bellingrath.org
(334)973-2217

Montgomery

April 6-8
🌿 Alabama Garden Festival
Recommended for families. A festival to celebrate spring with entertainment, gardening
seminars, a marketplace with fifty vendors,
plant swaps and other activities for garden
enthusiasts of all ages. Food available on
site. Annual event, now in its 2nd year.
Hours: noon- 6pm Fri; 8am-6pm Sat;

Remember that schedules do change.

noon-5pm Sun
Fee: $5; $3 ages 12-18; under 12 free
Jasmine Hill Gardens & Outdoor Museum,
3001 Jasmine Hill Road, Wetumpka, AL
Mail: PO Box 210792, Montgomery, AL
36121-0792
Web: www.jasminehill.org
(334)567-6463

FLORIDA

Belleview

February 23-25
🪷 **Florida Gourd Workshops & Show**
An exhibition and judged show in more than
100 categories of both natural and decorated gourds, plus gourd crafting workshops
and a sale of crafted and natural gourds,
gourd crafts, books and crafting tools from
vendor booths adjacent to the exhibits.
Held under three big tents adjacent to a
popular flea market. Annual event.
Hours: Workshops only 8am-5pm Fri; workshops & show 8am-5pm Sat; show only
9am-3pm Sun
Fee: Show free; workshop fees vary
Market of Marion, Highway 441, 2 miles
south of town, Belleview, FL
Contact: **Florida Gourd Society**, 650 SW
Bird Avenue, Keystone Heights, FL 32656
Web: grove.ufl.edu/~klewis/gourdshow.htm
(352)473-0291

Bradenton

March 31 - April 1
🪷 **Manatee River Garden Club Show**
This year's theme, "It's Showtime." A judged
standard flower show of hundreds of horticulture entries and floral designs. Show extends
outdoors into Lewis Park with educational
exhibits, demonstrations, lectures and vendors. Hot or cold picnic lunches available for
purchase. Held in Old Fogertyville in the historic section of Bradenton.
Hours: 10am-5pm; open earlier to seniors
in assisted living facilities
Fee: Free
The Garden Center, 3120 First Avenue
West, Bradenton, FL 34205
E-mail: w5thglyf@earthlink.com
(941)752-9758

Coral Gables

March 31 - April 1
🪷 **Bromeliad Show & Sale**
A show and sale of these decorative orna-
mentals from the mountains, coastal areas
and rain forests of Central and South
America. Sponsored by the Bromeliad
Society of South Florida. Annual event.
Hours: 9:30am-4:30pm
Fee: Regular admission
Fairchild Tropical Garden, 10901 Old
Cutler Road, Coral Gables, FL 33156
Web: www.ftg.org
(305)667-1651

April 7-8
🪷 **Heliconia Sale**
A plant sale of heliconia, banana and
calathea presented by the Heliconia Society
of South Florida.
Hours: 9:30am-4:30pm
Fee: Regular admission
Fairchild Tropical Garden *See earlier list-
ing in this section.*

Be sure to check with the sponsor in advance.

Web: www.ftg.org
(305)667-1651

May 12-13
🌺 Flowering Tree Show & Sale
Display and sale of a wide range of flowering trees with trees in the Gardens as a reference. Sponsored by the Tropical Flowering Tree Society. Annual event.
Hours: 9:30am-4:30pm
Fee: Regular admission
Fairchild Tropical Garden *See earlier listing in this section.*
Web: www.ftg.org
(305)667-1651

May 25-27
🌺 Cactus & Succulent Show & Sale
A show and sale of uncommon, unusual and interesting cactus and succulent species. Presented by The South Florida Cactus and Succulent Society.
Hours: 9:30am-4:30pm
Fee: Regular admission
Fairchild Tropical Garden *See earlier listing in this section.*
Web: www.ftg.org
(305)667-1651

June 2-3
🌺 Fern Society Show & Sale
A show and sale of rare and limited collected species of ferns. Presented by the South Florida Fern Society. Annual event.
Hours: 9:30am-4:30pm
Fee: Regular admission
Fairchild Tropical Garden *See earlier listing in this section.*
Web: www.ftg.org
(305)667-1651

June 10
🌺 Bamboo Show & Sale
A chance to view the Garden's extensive bamboo collection, then select from many species for planting in home gardens. Annual event.
Hours: 9:30am-4:30pm
Fee: Regular admission
Fairchild Tropical Garden *See earlier listing in this section.*
Web: www.ftg.org
(305)667-1651

July 14-15
🌺 International Mango Festival
A celebration of the mango with tastings of cultivars and mango-inspired concoctions, a display of 150 cultivars from around the world, a tree sale, workshops, music, plus Mangoville with mango inspired art, food and gift items. Mango brunch at 11am Sunday by reservation and live auction Sunday night at 5:30pm. Annual event.
Hours: Opens 9:30am Sat; trees sell out quickly
Fee: Regular admission
Fairchild Tropical Garden *See earlier listing in this section.*
Web: www.ftg.org
(305)667-1651

September 22-23
🌺 Aroid Society Show & Sale
A show and sale of these exotic jungle plants. Presented by the International Aroid Society. Annual event.
Hours: 9:30am-4:30pm
Fee: Regular admission
Fairchild Tropical Garden *See earlier listing in this section.*

Remember that schedules do change.

Web: www.ftg.org
(305)667-1651

October 6-7
🌺 **Hibiscus Show & Sale**
A show and sale of these beautiful flowering shrubs. Annual event.
Hours: 9:30am-4:30pm
Fee: Regular admission
Fairchild Tropical Garden *See earlier listing in this section.*
Web: www.ftg.org
(305)667-1651

October 13-14
🌺 **Bonsai Society Show & Sale**
An exhibition of these sculpted miniature trees, sale of supplies and plant materials, lectures and demonstrations. Presented by the Bonsai Society of Miami, bonsaiofmiami@juno.com. Annual event.
Hours: 9:30am-4:30pm
Fee: Regular admission
Fairchild Tropical Garden *See earlier listing in this section.*
Web: www.ftg.org
(305)667-1651

November 3-4
🌺 **International Palm Society Show & Sale**
One of the largest sales of rare and exotic palms in the country. Sponsored by the South Florida Chapter of the International Palm Society. Annual event.
Hours: 9:30am-4:30pm
Fee: Regular admission
Fairchild Tropical Garden *See earlier listing in this section.*
Web: www.ftg.org
(305)667-1651

November 10-11
🌺 **Ramble: A Garden Festival**
Recommended for families. Exhibits and sales of more than 15,000 plants including culinary herbs, palms, flowering trees, heliconias, bromeliads and fruit trees. Garden Marketplace, food and children's activities. Annual event, now in its 61st year.
Hours: 9:30am-4:30pm
Fee: Regular admission
Fairchild Tropical Garden *See earlier listing in this section.*
Web: www.ftg.org
(305)667-1651

Daytona Beach
45 miles east of Orlando

March 15-18
🌺 **Daytona Beach Garden Show** ★★★
One of Florida's largest garden shows with professionally-landscaped theme gardens, the juried award-winning "Everybody's Flower Show" presented by the Halifax District of the Council of Garden Clubs, presentations by nationally renowned horticulturists and floral designers, new plant exhibition, interactive chidren's discovery center and a marketplace with more than 120 vendors. Sponsored by The Daytona Beach News-Journal. Annual event.
Hours: 10am-5:30pm Thurs-Sat; 11am-5pm Sun
Fee: $3; children under 12 free
Ocean Center, 101 North Atlantic Ave (Route A1A), Daytona Beach, FL
Contact: **Daytona Beach Garden Show**, 901 6th Street, Daytona Beach, FL 32117
Web: www.daytonabeachgardenshow.com
(904)252-1511

Be sure to check with the sponsor in advance.

Fort Pierce

May 5
♨ May Fest
A celebration of spring, including tours of the Gardens, a spring plant sale of shrubs, perennials, vines, ground covers, herbs, native plants, butterfly plants and trees, plus a bargain bazaar of treasures to be recycled and put to use. Proceeds support the operation of the Gardens. Annual event.
Hours: 9am-3pm
Fee: Regular admission
Heathcote Botanical Gardens, 210 Savannah Road, Fort Pierce, FL 34982
E-mail: hbg@ircc
(561)464-4672

November 17-18
♨ Garden Festival
Recommended for families. Plant sales from vendors around Florida offering trees, shrubs, orchids, bromeliads, gingers, butterfly plants, vines, ferns, native plants, herbs, bonsai and African violets, plus garden-related books, statuary and garden accessories. Includes demonstrations, children's activities, educational and conservation booths, food and music. Annual event, now in its 14th year.
Hours: 9am-5pm Sat; 9am-3pm Sun
Fee: Regular admission
Heathcote Botanical Gardens *See earlier listing in this section.*
E-mail: hbg@ircc
(561)464-4672

December
♨ Christmas in the Gardens
Recommended for families. Open evenings at the Gardens filled with natural beauty, music and holiday lights. Heathcote House decorated for the season and light refreshments available. Annual event, now in its 4th year. Contact sponsor for exact dates.
Fee: Regular admission
Heathcote Botanical Gardens *See earlier listing in this section.*
E-mail: hbg@ircc
(561)464-4672

Gainesville

March 24-25
♨ Spring Garden Festival
Recommended for families. Plants, garden-related merchandise, arts and crafts for sale, along with horticultural seminars, live entertainment, children's activities and food. Annual event, now in its 11th year.
Kanapaha Botanical Gardens, 4700 SW 58th Drive, Gainesville, FL 32608
Web: hammock.ifas.ufl.edu/kanapaha
(352)372-4981

Homestead
35 miles south of Miami

January 13-14
♨ Redland Natural Arts Festival
Recommended for families. A celebration of Florida's pioneer spirit in which everything sold must be hand-made of natural materials. Features displays and sales by local artisans, artists and gardeners. Includes sales of tropical fruit trees, flowers and ethnic foods, plus puppetry, folk music and natural arts demonstrations. Annual event.
Hours: 10am-5pm
Fruit & Spice Park, 24801 SW 187th

Remember that schedules do change.

Avenue, Homestead, FL 33031
Web: www.co.miami-dade.fl.us/parks/
fruitandspice.htm
(305)247-5727

March 3-4
ℒ Asian-American Arts Festival
Recommended for families. A festival with
Asian food, entertainment and products on
display and for sale, plus a sale of tropical
fruit and flowering trees. Sponsored by the
Asian American Federation. Annual event.
Dates tentative. Call to confirm.
Fruit & Spice Park *See earlier listing in this
section.*
Web: www.co.miami-dade.fl.us/parks/
fruitandspice.htm
(305)247-5727

Jacksonville

February 22-25
ℒ Jacksonville Home & Patio Show
A major event in the Jacksonville area.
Includes gardens on the concourse, a land-
scaped centerpiece home, floral design
seminars and a children's area, plus home-
related displays and exhibits.
Prime F. Osborn III Convention Center,
1000 Water Street, Jacksonville, FL
Contact: **dmg world media, inc.**, 8400 Bay
Meadows Way, Suite 8, Jacksonville,
FL 32256
(800)645-7798 or (904)730-3356

Key West

Late January - Early March
ℒ House & Garden Tours
Two-day tours, each featuring five private

homes and gardens selected for historic
value or unique design features.
Annual event.
Old Island Restoration Foundation, PO
Box 689, Key West, FL 33041
(305)294-9501

Lake Buena Vista

April 20-22
ℒ Florida Federation of Garden Clubs
Flower Show
A competitive show with many entries in
both horticulture and design, plus a youth
section, special exhibits, educational
booths and participation by many plant
societies and clubs. Part of the month-long
Flower and Garden Festival at Epcot.
Fee: Free; donations welcome
Epcot Center, Lake Buena Vista, FL
Contact: **Florida Federation of Garden
Clubs**, 1400 South Denning Drive, Winter
Park, FL 32789
Web: www.ffgc.org
(407)647-7016

Late April - Early June
ℒ Epcot International Flower &
Garden Festival
Demonstrations, guest speakers and work-
shops against a backdrop hundreds of flow-
er beds, millions of blossoms and topiary
displays. Annual event.
Walt Disney Epcot Center, Lake Buena
Vista, FL
Mail: PO Box 10,000, Lake Buena Vista,
FL 32830
Web: www.disneyworld.com
(407)938-3900

Be sure to check with the sponsor in advance.

Lake Wales

February
℘ International Carillon Festival
World-renowned carillonneurs performing on the famous 57-bell Bok Tower carillon. Lectures by guest artists and garden walks, plus a special moonlight recital one evening. Annual event. Contact sponsor for exact dates.
Bok Tower Gardens, 1151 Tower Boulevard, Lake Wales, FL 33853
Web: www.boktower.org
(863)676-1408

Miami

March 2-4
℘ Miami International Orchid Show ★★★
This year's theme, "Orchid Odyssey 2001." A major show presented by the South Florida Orchid Society and attended by orchidists from all over the world, with exhibits, lectures, demonstrations and materials for sale. One of the largest orchid shows in the country.
Hours: 10am-8pm Fri-Sat; 10am-6pm Sun
Coconut Grove Convention Center, 2700 South Bayshore Drive, Coconut Grove, FL
Contact: **South Florida Orchid Society**, 10801 SW 124th Street, Miami, FL 33176
Web: sforchid@bellsouth.net
(305)255-3656

March 17-18
℘ Metropolitan Miami Flower Show
A judged show featuring floral designs, horticultural displays, lectures, vendors, music and walks of Simpson Park Hammock, the only natural hammock remaining in Miami. Annual event, now in its 46th year.
Hours: 10am-4pm
Fee: $5; children under 12 free
Charles Torrey Simpson Garden Center, 55 SW 17th Road, Miami, FL
Contact: **Metropolitan Miami Flower Show**, 55 SW 17 Road, Miami, FL 33129
(305)271-0735

June 2-3
℘ Royal Poinciana Festival
Recommended for families. A city-wide event coinciding with the blooming of the flame-colored blossoms of the Royal Poinciana trees. Features a large plant sale that includes Royal Poinciana seedlings, plant-related lectures and a trolley tour of trees. Funded by the City of Miami Beautification Committee. Annual event.
Annual Royal Poinciana Festival, 2472 SW 27 Terrace, Miami, FL 33133
(305)859-9455

Mount Dora
30 miles from Orlando

November 3-4
℘ Mount Dora Plant & Garden Fair
Exhibits by professional growers and skilled artisans at the Fair's large new site along the shore of Lake Dora. Features everything from alocasias to zamia and stepping stones to gazebos. One of the biggest garden shows in central Florida. Annual event, now in its 7th year.
Hours: 9am-5pm
Fee: Free
Gilbert Park, The lakefront at Tremain Street (off US Highway 441), Mount Dora, FL

Remember that schedules do change.

Contact: **Mt. Dora Library Association**,
37315 Beach Drive, Dona Vista, FL 32784
Web: www.mt-dora.com
(352)357-4116

Naples

October 11-14
☙ Orchid Showcase
An exhibit of hundreds of exotic orchids displayed throughout the hotel lobby, plus daily tours of the Orchid House, home to over 5,000 orchids.
The Naples Beach Hotel & Golf Club, 851 Gulf Shore Blvd, North, Naples, FL 33940
Web: www.naplesbeachhotel.com
(800)237-7600

Ocala

March 10-11
☙ Marion County Master Gardeners Spring Festival
A large festival featuring garden tours, seminars, specialty garden products, plant sales and education booths.
Hours: 9am-5pm
Fee: Free
Agriculture Center, 2232 NE Jacksonville Road, Ocala, FL
Contact: **Marion County Master Gardeners**, Agricultural Center, 2232 NE Jacksonville Road, Ocala, FL 34470
Web: www.marioncountyfl.org/coopext/
(352)620-3440

October 13
☙ Marion County Master Gardeners Fall Gathering
Many unusual plants donated by Master

Gardeners and local businesses available at very reasonable prices. Usually sells out by noon. Annual event, now in its 6th year.
Hours: Opens 9am
Fee: Free
Marion County Master Gardeners See earlier listing in this section.
Web: www.marioncountyfl.org/coopext/
(352)620-3440

Orlando

January 20-21
☙ Central Florida Camellia Society Show
Award-winning blooms on display in one of the largest camellia collections in the southeast.
Hours: 9am-5pm
Fee: Free entry to this event
Harry P. Leu Gardens, 1920 North Forest Avenue, Orlando, FL 32803
Web: www.leugardens.org
(407)246-2620

March 11
☙ Herbal Renaissance
A celebration of herbs with vendors, seminars, food, music, and demonstrations. A fundraiser for the Herb Society of Central Florida to endow scholarship at community college.
Harry P. Leu Botanical Gardens, Orlando, FL
Contact: **Herb Society of Central Florida**, PO Box 11183, Orlando, FL 32803
(407)897-3333

March 24-25
☙ Leu Gardens Spring Plant Sale
Vendors throughout the Gardens selling

Be sure to check with the sponsor in advance.

plants, plant-related products and outdoor accessories. Growing tips from experts. Annual event.
Hours: 9am-5pm
Fee: Free entry to this event
Harry P. Leu Gardens *See earlier listing in this section.*
Web: www.leugardens.org
(407)246-2620

March 30 - April 1
❧ Central Florida Home & Garden Show
Central Florida's largest consumer home and garden show with nearly 400 exhibitors. Features a landscape competition plus six seminar speakers a day, including master gardeners and local celebrities. Annual event.
Orange County Convention Center, 9800 International Drive, Hall C, Orlando, FL
Contact: **Home Builders Association of Mid Florida**, 544 Mayo Avenue, Maitland, FL 32751
Web: www.comehomeorlando.com
(407)629-9242

May 12
❧ Daylily Show
A show presented by the Central Florida Hemerocallis Society. Includes a sale of daylilies. Annual event.
Hours: 9am-5pm
Fee: Free entry to this event
Harry P. Leu Gardens *See earlier listing in this section.*
Web: www.leugardens.org
(407)246-2620

August 18
❧ Orchid Auction & Show

A show presented by the Central Florida Orchid Society. Annual event.
Hours: 1pm-5pm
Fee: Free entry to this event
Harry P. Leu Gardens *See earlier listing in this section.*
Web: www.leugardens.org
(407)246-2620

December 7-9
❧ Winter Holidays
Recommended for families. Holiday decorations in the museum, luminarias in the Gardens, music, visits by Santa and carolers. Annual event.
Harry P. Leu Gardens *See earlier listing in this section.*
Web: www.leugardens.org
(407)246-2620

Palatka
50 miles from Jacksonville

March 3-4, 9-11
❧ Florida Azalea Festival
Recommended for families. A week of events along the banks of the St. Johns River against a backdrop of azaleas in full bloom. Lots of entertainment, arts, crafts and other activities. Annual event, now in its 56th year.
Hours: Gates open 10am
Fee: Free
Banks of St. Johns River, 100 St. Johns Avenue, Palatka, FL
Contact: **Florida Azalea Festival**, PO Box 152, Palatka, FL 32178
Web: www.flazaleafest.com
(904)326-4001

Remember that schedules do change.

Pensacola

February 16-18
⚘ **Pensacola Home & Garden Show**
A regional show featuring several show gardens, seminars and products and services for home and garden.
Hours: 11am-9pm Fri-Sat; 11am-6pm Sun
Fee: $6
Pensacola Civic Center, 201 East Gregory Street, Pensacola, FL
Contact: **Exposition Enterprises, Inc.**, PO Box 430, Pinson, AL 35126
E-mail: expoei@wwisp.com
(800)226-3976 or (205)680-0234

April 6-8
⚘ **Emerald Coast Flower & Garden Festival**
A festival featuring a standard flower show, over fifty vendors with plants and garden-related items, lectures, demonstrations, exhibits and refreshments. Coincides with Pensacola Junior College's Spring Fling. Annual event.
Fee: Free
Pensacola Junior College, Milton Campus, Milton, FL
Contact: **Pensacola Federation of Garden Clubs, Inc.**, 1850 North 9th Avenue, Pensacola, FL 32503
Web: www.floridaplants.com/pensacola.htm
(850)432-6095 Mon, Wed, Fri 10am-3pm

May 20
⚘ **Secret Gardens of the Emerald Coast**
A self-guided tour of twelve gardens in the Pensacola area.

Pensacola Federation of Garden Clubs, Inc. *See earlier listing in this section.*
Web:
www.floridaplants.com/pensacola.htm
(850)432-6095 Mon, Wed, Fri 10am-3pm

Punta Gorda

December 7-8
⚘ **Punta Gorda Home & Garden Show**
A unique judged show held at four private homes, each of which competes with six elements such as entry way, table arrangement, wreath and tree. All arrangements made of natural material and ribbons and judge's comments on display. Simultaneous horticultural competition and educational exhibits in the Church hall. Held in the picturesque Punta Gorda, home of Harry Goulding, the "father" of hibiscus. Annual event. Dates tentative. Call to confirm.
Hours: noon-5pm
United Methodist Church, West Marion Avenue, Punta Gorda, FL
Contact: **The Punta Gorda Garden Club, Inc.**, 3438 Pennyroyal Road, Port Charlotte, FL 33953
Web: www.pggc.org
(941)764-0558

Sarasota

April 7-8
⚘ **Sarasota Garden Club Flower Show**
A judged flower show with horticultural, floral design and educational exhibits and youth gardener displays. Held on the property of the Sarasota Garden Club which includes a one acre botanical garden with butterfly garden and enclosed pond garden.

Be sure to check with the sponsor in advance.

Annual event, now in its 64th year.
Hours: 1-5pm Sat; noon-5pm Sun
Fee: $3.50
Sarasota Garden Club Center, 1131 Blvd
of the Arts, Sarasota, FL 34236
(941)955-0875

April 21-22
🌿 Sarasota Bromeliad Society
Show & Sale
This year's theme, "2001 A Bromeliad
Odyssey!" Bromeliads on display and for
sale in the Activities Center, plus a rare
plant auction. Refreshments available.
Annual event, now in its 21st year.
Hours: 10am-5pm
Fee: Regular admission
Marie Selby Botanical Gardens, 811
South Palm Avenue, Sarasota, FL 34236
Web: www.selby.org
(941)366-5731

November 17-19
🌿 Fall Plant Fair
Thousands of native and tropical plants for
indoor and outdoor landscaping. Annual
event.
Marie Selby Botanical Gardens *See earlier*
listing in this section.
Web: www.selby.org
(941)366-5731

Late November - December
🌿 Jingle in the Jungle
Recommended for families. Thousands of
live poinsettias, an 18-foot Christmas tree,
lots of entertainment and holiday music.
Annual event.
Sarasota Jungle Gardens, 3701 Bayshore
Road, Sarasota, FL 34234

Web: www.sarasotajunglegardens.com
(941)355-5305

December
🌿 Holiday Celebration & Gardens
by Candlelight
Recommended for families. Seasonal floral
displays on the grounds and in the
Museum. Evening hours on the opening two
nights, with luminarias in the gardens,
entertainment, food and fun for all ages.
Annual event.
Marie Selby Botanical Gardens *See earlier*
listing in this section.
Web: www.selby.org
(941)366-5731

Southwest Ranches
Near Weston, Davie

May 12
🌿 Rare Fruit Tree Spring Sale
Spring sale of rare fruit trees for South
Florida and subtropics including mango,
avocado, tropical cherries and others.
Hours: 9:30am-4pm
Fee: Free
Rare Fruit and Vegetable Council
Research Center, 5101 SW 208th Lane,
Southwest Ranches, FL
Contact: **Rare Fruit & Vegetable Council**,
4951 SW 193 Lane, Ft. Lauderdale,
FL 33332
E-mail: mbasile@newssun.med.miami.edu
(954)748-9841

Remember that schedules do change.

October
⚘ Rare Fruit Tree & Vegetable Plant Sale

Sale of rare and unusual subtropical fruit trees including many cultivars of mango, avocado, lychee, longan, ingas, sapotes and tropical cherries. Vegetable seedlings for fall planting in South Florida. Cultural advice and examples of specimen trees on property. Contact sponsor for exact date.
Fee: Free
Rare Fruit and Vegetable Council Research Center, 5101 SW 208th Lane, Southwest Ranches, FL
Contact: **Rare Fruit & Vegetable Council**
See earlier listing in this section.
E-mail: mbasile@newssun.med.miami.edu
(954)748-9841

St. Augustine
30 miles from Jackksonville

March 30 - April 1
⚘ An EPIC Celebration of Spring

A festival with major events on each day. A gathering of St. Augustine's finest restaura- teurs and tastings of their signature dishes on Friday, an expo with noted speakers and exhibits by growers and nurseries from all over Florida on Saturday and Sunday, and a tour of historic inns and gardens on Sunday.
Hours: Tastings 5:30-9pm Fri; Expo 9am- 5pm Sat, 10am-4pm Sun; Tour 2-6pm Sun
Fee: Tastings $1; Expo $5; Tour $10
Special Events Field, Castillo Drive behind Visitors Center, St. Augustine, FL
Contact: **EPIC Community Services**, 88 Riberia Street, Suite 300, St. Augustine, FL 32084

Web: userpages.aug.com/epic/
(904)829-2273

Stuart
35 miles from Palm Beach

March 24-25
⚘ The Garden Club of Stuart Flower Show

A judged show of more than seventy-five floral arrangements by local club members on view throughout the Museum. On the grounds, a sale of plants and garden items by local nurseries and a sale of art work by the Jensen Beach Art League. Lecture and luncheon available by reservation. Cosponsored by the Garden Club of Stuart and the Historical Society of Martin County.
Hours: 10am-4pm
Fee: $3 donation requested
Elliott Museum, 825 NE Ocean Blvd, Hutchinson Island, Stuart, FL 34996
Web: www.goodnature.org/elliottmuseum/
(561)225-1961

Tallahassee

March
⚘ Maclay Garden Tour

A tour of five to seven private plantations and gardens in the area, plus a guest speaker and picnic. Sponsored by Friends of Maclay State Gardens. Annual event. Contact sponsor for exact date.
Alfred B. Maclay State Gardens, 3540 Thomasville Road, Tallahassee, FL 32308
Web: www.ssnow.com/maclay/
(850)487-4115

Be sure to check with the sponsor in advance.

Tampa

October 13-14

Fall Plant Festival

The largest plant sale in the Tampa Bay area with more than sixty specialty clubs, societies nurseries and other vendors participating. Often includes judged Society shows. Refreshments available.

University of South Florida Botanical Garden, Pine & Alumni Drives (SW corner of campus), Tampa, FL

Mail: 4202 East Fowler, SCA 238, Tampa, FL 33620

Web: www.cas.usf.edu/envir_sci_policy /botanical/gardenfaq.html

(813)974-2329

Vero Beach

January 10

Garden Symposium

A symposium sponsored by the Northern Trust Bank to benefit the Garden. Annual event, now in its 4th year.

Hours: Registration 9:15am; seminar 10am-2pm

Fee: $60

Riomar Bay Yacht Club, Highway A1A, Vero Beach, FL

Contact: **McKee Botanical Garden**, 350 South US Highway 1, Vero Beach, FL 32962

Web: www.mckeegarden.org

(561)794-0601

West Palm Beach

February 23-25

Palm Beach Tropical Flower & Garden Show ★★★

Recommended for families. This year's theme, "A Symphony of Flowers." Brings together nationally-known lecturers, plant societies and Florida's top nurseries and landscape designers in a display of tropical gardening staged on 8.5 acres along the intracoastal waterway. Includes a major flower show competition, musical and dance performances, a Garden Marketplace, horticultural demonstrations, an educational display from Mounts Botanical Garden and a children's gardening activity area. Annual event.

Hours: 10am-6pm

Fee: $10; $8 seniors; children under 12 free; reduced rates available in advance

Flagler Drive, Intracoastal Waterway between Evernia & Banyan, West Palm Beach, FL

Contact: **The Horticulture Society of South Florida**, 464 Fern Street, West Palm Beach, FL 33401

Web: www.palmbeachflowershow.org

(561)655-5522

March 11

Spring Family Festival

Recommended for families. A day of fun and education for children in the Garden. Children's gardening classes, pony rides, bounce house, ladybug release, food and refreshments. Sponsored by the Friends of Mounts Botanical Garden. Date tentative. Call to confirm.

Fee: Free

Remember that schedules do change.

Mounts Botanical Garden, 531 North Military Trail, West Palm Beach, FL 33415
Web: www.mounts.org
(561)233-1749

April 28-29
🏛 **Mounts Botanical Garden Spring Plant Sale**
A sale of hard-to-find plants at reasonable prices. Includes orchids, tropical plants, flowering trees, palms, bromeliads and herbs. Sponsored by the Friends of the Mounts Botanical Garden. Annual event.
Mounts Botanical Garden *See earlier listing in this section.*
Web: www.mounts.org
(561)233-1749

October 21
🏛 **Fall Family Festival**
Recommended for families. A day of fun and education in the Garden with children's gardening classes, pony rides, bounce house, ladybug release, food and refreshments.
Mounts Botanical Garden *See earlier listing in this section.*
Web: www.mounts.org
(561)233-1749

Winter Haven
Southwest of Orlando and east of Tampa

Thanksgiving - New Year's
🏛 **Garden of Lights Holiday Festival**
Recommended for families. Millions of twinkling lights throughout the gardens with over 200 animated scenes, a Poinsettia Festival and holiday concerts. Annual event.
Hours: Extended to 9pm

Fee: Regular admission
Cypress Gardens, 2641 South Lake Summit Drive, Winter Haven, FL
Mail: PO Box 1, Winter Haven, FL 33884
Web: www.cypressgardens.com
(800)282-2123

GEORGIA
Athens

January - November
🏛 **Garden Rambles**
A series of guided garden tours held once a month, usually on the third Saturday of the month.
Fee: Free
State Botanical Garden of Georgia, 2450 South Milledge Avenue, Athens, GA 30605
Web: www.uga.edu/botgarden/
(706)542-1244

January 31
🏛 **Wildflower Symposium**
A wildflower symposium sponsored by The Garden Clubs of Georgia, The State Botanical Garden and the Georgia Plant Conservation Alliance.
State Botanical Garden of Georgia *See earlier listing in this section.*
Web: www.uga.edu/botgarden/
(706)542-1244

March - May, Mid September - October
🏛 **Open Garden Days**
Open garden days every Friday and Saturday during these months at the country's largest producer of hellebores. Thousands of hellebores, plus collections of

Be sure to check with the sponsor in advance.

southeast hostas, perennials, ferns, native wildflowers and one of the largest collections of conifers in the southeast which includes 300 kinds of dwarf conifers.
Hours: 10am-4pm
Fee: Free
Piccadilly Farm, 1971 Whippoorwill Road, Bishop, GA 30621
(706)769-6516

March 2-3
✿ Hellebore Day
A nationally-known sale of hellebores with thousands of clumps to choose from and experts on hand in the display gardens to help with selection. Annual event, now in its 9th year.
Hours: 10am-4pm
Fee: Free
Piccadilly Farm *See earlier listing in this section.*
(706)769-6516

April 7
✿ Spring Plant Sale
A good selection of annuals, perennials, roses, shrubs, herbs, ferns, ornamentals and vegetables, including many hard-to-find and native species. Annual event.
Fee: Free
State Botanical Garden of Georgia *See earlier listing in this section.*
Web: www.uga.edu/botgarden/
(706)542-1244

October 6
✿ Fall Plant Sale
A plant sale featuring Garden grown herbs, cool-season annuals, perennials, trees and shrubs. Annual event.
Fee: Free
State Botanical Garden of Georgia *See earlier listing in this section.*
Web: www.uga.edu/botgarden/
(706)542-1244

October 9
✿ Perennial Symposium
A symposium with expert speakers and panelists timed to the fall planting season.
State Botanical Garden of Georgia *See earlier listing in this section.*
Web: www.uga.edu/botgarden/
(706)542-1244

December 2
✿ Holiday Open House
A special celebration of the holidays with poinsettias, topiary and thousands of white lights in the Conservatory.
State Botanical Garden of Georgia *See earlier listing in this section.*
Web: www.uga.edu/botgarden/
(706)542-1244

Atlanta

February 3
✿ Perennial Symposium
Day-long symposium cosponsored by the Georgia Perennial Plant Association and the Atlanta Botanical Garden. Speakers include Pamela Harper, Peter Loewer, Bill Funkhouser and Barbara Ashmun. Contact the Education Department to register. Annual event, now in its 17th year.
Hours: 8:30am-3:30pm
Atlanta Botanical Garden, 1345 Piedmont Avenue NE, Atlanta, GA 30309

Remember that schedules do change.

Web: www.atlantabotanicalgarden.org
(404)876-5859

February 8-11
⚘ Atlanta Garden & Patio Show
A large regional show that features live gardens by some of Atlanta's most gifted master gardeners, landscape architects and horticulturists, presentations by nationally known celebrities and gardening experts, children's sessions on environment-related subjects and a large marketplace with hundreds of garden products and services for sale. Held in the beautiful space of the Cobb Galleria Centre. Annual event.
Fee: $8; $7 seniors; $2 children 7-12; children under 7 free; no charge for parking
Cobb Galleria Centre, Two Galleria Parkway, intersection of Cobb Parkway/US 41 and I 285 (across from Cumberland Mall), Atlanta, GA
Contact: **Atlanta Garden & Patio Show**, 1130 Hightower Trail, Atlanta, GA 30350-6202
Web: www.atlantahomeshow.com
(770)998-9800

February 21-25
⚘ Southeastern Flower Show ★★★
Features professionally landscaped gardens, competitions, amateur and professional floral displays, education gardens, horticulture exhibits, a 100-booth marketplace, bookstore, nationally know speakers and a food court. One of the largest juried, non-profit flower and gardening events in the U.S.
Hours: 9:30am-6:30pm Wed-Thurs; 9:30am-8:30pm Fri-Sat; 9:30am-6pm Sun
Fee: $15; $5 youth (4-16); children under

4 free; $11 two-day ticket; $35 guided tour; $11 advance; $3 parking
Atlanta Expo Center, 3650 Jonesboro Road SE, Atlanta, GA
Contact: **Southeastern Flower Show**, 1475 Peachtree Street NE, Atlanta, GA 30309
Web: www.flowershow.org
(404)888-5638

April 6-8
⚘ Atlanta Dogwood Festival
Recommended for families. A springtime celebration with more than 200 artists in the Park, a children's corner, competitions, activities and live music among the dogwood blossoms. Proceeds support the Magic Garden program. Annual event.
Fee: Free
Piedmont Park, east on 10th Street off 75 NORS (deadends in Park), Atlanta, GA
Contact: **The Atlanta Dogwood Festival**, 4 Executive Park Drive, Suite 1217, Atlanta, GA 30329
Web: www.dogwood.org
(404)329-0501

April 27-29
⚘ Druid Hills Home & Garden Tour
A tour of the Druid Hills neighborhood and Park, the last project by designer Frederick Law Olmsted. A restoration of the Park is currently underway. Annual event.
Druid Hills Home & Garden Tour, 1390 Vilenah Lane NE, Atlanta, GA 30307
(404)523-3422; (404)524-8687 recorded info

May 12-13
⚘ Gardens for Connoisseurs Tour
A Mother's Day weekend tour of private gar-

Be sure to check with the sponsor in advance.

dens in the Atlanta area. Annual event.
Atlanta Botanical Garden, 1345 Piedmont
Avenue NE, Atlanta, GA 30309
Web: www.atlantabotanicalgarden.org
(404)876-5859

May 12-13
❦ Greater Atlanta Rose Society Show & Sale

Hundreds of award winning roses exhibited
by amateur rose growers from the
Southeast. Includes modern, antique and
miniature roses on display and for sale.
Consulting rosarians will be on hand to
answer rose culture questions. Annual
event.
Atlanta Botanical Garden *See earlier listing in this section.*
Web: www.atlantabotanicalgarden.org
(404)876-5859

June
❦ Asian Cultural Experience

Recommended for families. A presentation
of the cultural contributions of Atlanta's
Chinese, Japanese, Korean, Indian,
Indonesian, Philippine and Taiwanese com-
munities. Craft pavilions and demonstrations of Chinese calligraphy, Ikebana,
Japanese embroidery, Oriental board games
and Bonsai, plus music, dancing, martial
arts, Asian cuisine and a Dragon Parade on
the Great Lawn. A chance to view plants
grown from seed collected in China by ABG
staff. Annual event. Contact sponsor for
exact dates.
Atlanta Botanical Garden *See earlier listing in this section.*
Web: www.atlantabotanicalgarden.org
(404)876-5859

December - Mid January, 2002
❦ Country Christmas

Recommended for families. Lights and seasonal displays throughout the Garden, plus
carolers, entertainment, activities and gift
items for sale. ABG's Christmas gift to the
city. Annual event.
Fee: Free entry to this event
Atlanta Botanical Garden *See earlier listing in this section.*
Web: www.atlantabotanicalgarden.org
(404)876-5859

Augusta

March 23-25
❦ Sacred Heart Garden Festival

Lectures, vendor sales and garden-related
activities, plus a tour of some of the finest
homes and gardens in Augusta, often called
"The Garden City." Annual event, now in its
10th year.
Sacred Heart Cultural Center, 1301
Greene Street, Augusta, GA 30901
Web: www.sacredheartaugusta.org
(706)826-4700

May
❦ Sacred Heart Garden Tour of Homes

A tour of some of the finest homes and gardens in Augusta's historic area and unique
suburban settings. Contact sponsor for
exact dates.
Hours: 11am-5pm
Fee: $15
Sacred Heart Cultural Center *See earlier
listing in this section.*
Web: www.sacredheartaugusta.org
(706)826-4700

Columbus

May 12
❦ Georgia Historic House & Garden Pilgrimage

A tour of eight historic properties and gardens, including Linwood Cemetery and the Columbus Museum's Frederick Olmsted Gardens. Lunch available at the Museum by reservation. Sponsored by the Garden Club of Georgia and benefits their programs. Annual event.

Historic House & Garden Tour, 2307 Hilton Ave, Columbus, GA 30906
Web: www.uga.edu/gardenclub/
(706)322-5753

Dahlonega

May 19-20
❦ Wildflower Festival of the Arts

Recommended for families. A festival featuring an Artist Marketplace with over seventy-five artists, a Wildflower Awareness Area, outdoor walking tours led by local naturalists, an indoor walking tour, award winning displays, lectures and talks by well known speakers, children's activities and an art raffle. Annual event.
Fee: Free
Historic Square & Community House, Dahlonega, GA
Contact: **Wildflower Festival of the Arts**, PO Box 1106, Dahlonega, GA 30533
Web: www.dahlonega.org/wildflower
(706)867-6829

Dunwoody

March 9-17
❦ Hard-to-Find Plant Sale

A preorder sale of exceptional and unique plants recommended by a panel of noted designers, national and local celebrities. An excellent collection of new introductions, native plants and others, selected for hardiness, uniqueness and beauty. Full list available from the Center in February and also available on their web site. Deadline for orders, March 9, and pickup on March 16-17.
Dunwoody Nature Center, 5343 Roberts Drive, Dunwoody, GA
Mail: PO Box 88834, Dunwoody, GA 30356
Web: www.dunwoodynature.org
(770)394-3322

May 18-20
❦ Garden Tour

A self-guided tour of seven private gardens and the Dunwoody Nature Center. Most homeowner-gardeners on hand to answer questions. Includes activities such as exhibits and speakers at the Center. Annual event.
Hours: 10am-3pm Fri; 10am-5pm Sat; 1-5pm Sun
Fee: $15
Dunwoody Nature Center *See earlier listing in this section.*
Web: www.dunwoodynature.org
(770)394-3322

Be sure to check with the sponsor in advance.

Fort Valley
30 miles from Macon

Early February
⚘ Camellia Festival
Recommended for families. A week of special events celebrating the camellia and featuring a tour of historic homes, a novice camellia show, workshops, an art show and activities for all ages and interests. Annual event. Contact sponsor for exact date.
Massee Lane Gardens, 100 Massee Lane, Fort Valley, GA 31030
Web: www.camellias-acs.com/ MasseeLane/index.html
(912)967-2358

Loganville

End of February
⚘ Rose Day at Vines
A day of rose-related activities, including planting and pruning demonstrations, expert speakers from the rose industry, a sale of roses and certified rosarians on hand to answer questions. Sponsored by the Greater Gwinnett Rose Society. Contact sponsor for exact date.
Vines Botanical Gardens, 3500 Oak Grove Road, Loganville, GA 30052
Web: www.vinesbotanicalgardens.com
(770)466-7532

Macon

March 16-25
⚘ Cherry Blossom Festival
Recommended for families. A city-wide celebration of the Yoshino Cherry Tree blossoms with riding tours, house and garden tours, the Federated Garden Club's Spring Garden Show, Ikebana flower arrangements at Woodruff House, concerts, theater productions, sports events, fireworks and the Hot Air Balloon Glow and Festival. Annual event, now in its 19th year.
Hours: 9am-9pm
Fee: Most events free
Macon Cherry Blossom Festival, 794 Cherry Street, Macon, GA 31201
Web: www.cherryblossom.com
(912)751-7429

Marietta

May - August
⚘ Backacher Garden Program Series
One Saturday a month from May to August, presentations by three Master Gardeners at different locations throughout the 2-acre Gardens, each focusing on one of the ten thematic garden areas. Presentations given three times, so visitors can rotate through the Gardens and hear them all. Sponsored by the Master Gardener Volunteers of Cobb County which maintain the Gardens. Annual event. Contact sponsor for exact dates.
Hours: 8am-noon
Fee: Free
Master Gardener Demonstration Gardens, behind Parks & Recreation Headquarters, 1792 County Services Parkway, Marietta, GA
Contact: **Cobb County Extension Service**, 1151 Whitlock Avenue, Marietta, GA 30064
Web: www.cobbextension.com
(770)528-4070

Remember that schedules do change.

Pine Mountain
1 hour southwest of Atlanta

February 2-4
☙ Southern Gardening Symposium
A three-day gardening event featuring experts on gardening in the South. For both amateur and professional gardeners. Annual event.
Fee: Special event fee
Callaway Gardens, US Highway 27, Pine Mountain, GA
Mail: PO Box 2000, Pine Mountain, GA 31822
Web: www.callawaygardens.com
(800)225-5292

March 22-25
☙ Plant Fair, Sale & Flower Show
A sale of rare and unique plants, plus a Southern Living seminar on Friday and educational programs throughout the weekend. Annual event.
Hours: 10am-6pm
Fee: Regular admission; preregistration for seminar required
Callaway Gardens *See earlier listing in this section.*
Web: www.callawaygardens.com
(800)225-5292

Mid March - Mid April
☙ Spring Celebration
Recommended for families. A celebration during spring bloom time at the Gardens, with azaleas and wildflowers in March and mountain laurel and rhododendron in April. Many family activities on the weekends including horse cart rides in the Vegetable

Garden and musical entertainment. Annual event.
Callaway Gardens *See earlier listing in this section.*
Web: www.callawaygardens.com
(800)225-5292

Mid November - December
☙ Fantasy in Lights
Recommended for families. A spectacular light display for the holidays. Annual event.
Callaway Gardens *See earlier listing in this section.*
Web: www.callawaygardens.com
(800)225-5292

Savannah

January 19-21
☙ The Low Country Living Home & Garden Show
A 10,000 square foot garden display, presentations by national celebrities such as Tom Silva of This Old House, plus a large vendors market of home and garden products.
The Savannah International Trade & Convention Center, Savannah, GA
Contact: **Show Technologies**, 711 Stoney Ridge Rd, Bulverde, TX 78163
Web: www.showtechnology.com
(830)980-4078

March 22-25
☙ Savannah Tour of Homes & Gardens ★★★
Four days of self-guided walking tours through Savannah's National Historic Landmark district with entry into remarkable 18th and 19th century homes and gardens.

Be sure to check with the sponsor in advance.

A variety of additional events, including a Low Country Tour, special luncheons and lectures, a Sunday dinner and garden tour at Mrs. Wilkes' Boarding House and a slide preview of Savannah's architectural history. Sponsored by the Episcopal Church Women of Christ Church and the Foundation. Annual event, now in its 66th year.
Fee: Tours from $30; special event fees vary
Historic Savannah Foundation, 18 Abercorn Street, Savannah, GA 31401
Web: www.savannahtourofhomes.org
(912)234-8054

April 27-28
🌿 **NOGS Hidden Gardens Tour**
A walking tour of eight private walled gardens in Savannah's famed historic district, north of Gaston Street (NOGS), plus the gardens of The Massie Heritage Center, restored and maintained by the Garden Club of Savannah. Tickets include a Southern-style tea at the Ward Anderson House. Annual event, now in its 26th year.
Hours: 10am-5pm; tea 2-5pm
Fee: $20; children under 10 free
Garden Club of Savannah, PO Box 13892, Savannah, GA 31416
(912)897-2177 or (912)238-0248

Thomasville

April 27-28
🌿 **Thomasville Garden Club Rose Show**
This year's theme, "Where Roses Reign, Southern Charm Abides." A judged show with horticulture, design and rose entries which attracts rose growers from Mississippi, Alabama, Georgia and Florida. Includes guided tours of the show, educa-

tion booths, participation by nurseries and florists, and vendors of garden-related products. One of the oldest and largest shows of its kind in the Southeast. Annual event, now in its 80th year.
Hours: 1:30-6pm Fri; 9:30am-5pm Sat
Fee: Donation
Thomasville Exchange Club Fairgrounds, 1103 Pavo Road, Hwy 122, Thomasville, GA
Contact: **Thomasville Garden Club**, PO Box 1273, Thomasville, GA 31799
E-mail: mtomlin@rose.net
(912)226-6649

Winterville
Near Athens

June 22-24
🌿 **Marigold Festival Day**
Recommended for families. A weekend celebration of many events at peak bloom of more than 7,000 marigolds planted all around this attractive town. Annual event.
Marigold Festival, PO Box 306, Winterville, GA 30683
Web: www.negia.net/~wintervi/
(706)742-8606

KENTUCKY

Clermont
25 miles south of Louisville

May 12
🌿 **Rare Plant Sale**
Hard to find and rare plants, trees and shrubs, all hardy to the region, tried and

tested at the Arboretum. Annual event.
Bernheim Arboretum & Research Forest,
Highway 245, Clermont, KY
Mail: PO Box 130, Clermont, KY 40110
Web: www.bernheim.org
(502)955-8512 or hotline (502)955-8822

October
⚘ Colorfest
Recommended for families. Nature and
craft exhibits, family activities, food, fun,
music and entertainment for everyone during peak fall color at the Arboretum. Annual
event. Contact sponsor for exact dates.
Bernheim Arboretum & Research Forest
See earlier listing in this section.
Web: www.bernheim.org
(502)955-8512 or hotline (502)955-8822

Lexington

April 14
⚘ Arbor Day Celebration
Recommended for families. A day of activi-
ties for everyone with speakers, children's
activities and information on the environ-
ment, ecology and gardening. Date tenta-
tive. Call to confirm.
Fee: Free
Arboreturm of the University of Kentucky,
Alumni Drive, Lexington, KY
Mail: University of Kentucky, 8 Gillis
Building, Lexington, KY 40506
E-mail: mfarr2@pop.uky.edu
(606)257-9339

Louisville

March 8-11
⚘ The Home Garden & Remodeling Show

A home show with a half dozen garden
areas and a wide array of products and ser-
vices for home and garden. Annual event,
now in its 51st year.
Hours: 5-10pm Thurs; noon-10pm Fri;
10am-10pm Sat; 11am-6pm Sun
Fee: $7; children under 12 free
Kentucky Fair & Exposition Center,
Louisville, KY
Contact: **Home Builder's Association of
Louisville**, 1000 North Hurstbourne
Parkway, Louisville, KY 40223
Web: www.hbal.com
(502)429-6000

April 5-7
⚘ National Daffodil Show
Show of the American Daffodil Society fea-
turing over 3000 daffodils from all over the
United States, England, Northern Ireland,
the Netherlands and Canada. Open to the
public on Saturday and Sunday. Held in
conjunction with the Society's convention.
Annual event.
Executive West, across from the airport,
Louisville, KY
Contact: **American Daffodil Society**, 4126
Winfield Road, Columbus, OH 43220
Web: www.daffodilusa.org
(614)481-4747

Paducah
150 miles from Nashville

January 13
⚘ Garden Gurus
Two lectures, one by R. William Thomas of
Longwood Gardens on Very Versatile Vines
and one by landscape architect and author
Richard Dube on Stonescaping the

Be sure to check with the sponsor in advance.

Landscape followed by an award-winning plants auction.
Hours: 1-6pm
Fee: $20
Cherry Civic Center, Park Avenue & H. C. Mathis Drive, Paducah, KY
Contact: **Purchase Area Master Gardeners Association**, 2705 Olivet Church Road, Paducah, KY 42001
E-mail: kkeeney@ca.uky.edu
(270)554-9520

Mid April
🌿 Lighted Dogwood Trail
Recommended for families. A two-week celebration of the blooming of the dogwoods that starts mid-April. Features an illuminated trail through more than twelve miles of Paducah's most beautiful residential areas. Begins with an evening kick-off reception at City Hall with music and refreshments followed by complimentary bus tours of the trail. Part of a spring celebration of the arts which includes a flower show, an art show, theater production, music and a bicycle tour. Annual event, now in its 38th year. Contact sponsor for exact dates.
Fee: Free
Paducah City Hall, 5th & Washington, Paducah, KY
Contact: **Paducah-McCracken County Visitors Bureau**, PO Box 90, Paducah, KY 42002
Web: www.paducah-tourism.org
800-PADUCAH (800-723-8224)

April 21
🌿 Master Gardeners Spring Plant Sale
Sale of heritage, common and new plants grown by Master Gardeners, many not available commercially. PAMGA members available to answer questions and conduct tours of the demonstration gardens.
Hours: 9am-2pm
Fee: Free
PAMG Research & Demonstration Garden
See earlier listing in this section.
E-mail: kkeeney@ca.uky.edu
(270)554-9520

May 12
🌿 Open Gate Garden Club Perennial Sale
A sale featuring member-grown perennial and shade plants. Funds used to support the Airport Viewing Garden at Fisher Road and US 60.
Hours: 10am-4pm
Fee: Free
Marie's Gifts, 922 Park Avenue, Paducah, KY
Contact: **Open Gate Garden Club**, 2015 Lone Oak Road, Paducah, KY 42003
E-mail: gardener@sunsix.infi.net
(502)554-4466 or (502)442-3089

June 25-30
🌿 McCracken County Fair
Includes the judged show of the Paducah Garden Club, plus competition of outstanding fruits and vegetables, harness racing, horse shows, variety show and midway. Sponsored by the Kiwanis Club to benefit local youth programs. Annual event, now in its 3rd year.
Carson Park Fairgrounds, Paducah, KY
Contact: **Paducah-McCracken County Visitors Bureau** *See earlier listing in this section.*
Web: www.paducah-tourism.org
800-PADUCAH (800-723-8224)

Remember that schedules do change.

LOUISIANA

Baton Rouge

March, May, June, October
🌿 Friends of Hilltop Garden Tours
A series of weekend tours of private gardens in Baton Rouge and surrounding area. Annual event. Contact sponsor for exact dates.
Friends of LSU Hilltop Arboretum, PO Box 82608, Baton Rouge, LA 70884
Web: hilltop.lsu.edu/hilltop/
(225)767-6916

March 31
🌿 Spring Plant Sale
A sale of herbs, roses, Louisiana iris, daylilies, hibiscus, bamboo, gingers, plus many garden accessories by more than two dozen vendors. Benefits the Garden. Annual event.
Hours: 8am-3pm
Fee: Free
Independence Park Botanic Garden, 7950 Independence Blvd, Baton Rouge, LA 70806
(225)928-2270 or (225)213-6405

Many

July 4
🌿 Independence Day Festival
Recommended for families. Arts and crafts, live entertainment and fireworks after dark to celebrate the 4th. Annual event.
Hodges Gardens & Wilderness, Highway 171 south of Many, Many, LA
Mail: PO Box 340, Florien, LA 71429
Web: www.hodgespark.com
(318)586-3523

Thanksgiving - December
🌿 Christmas Lights Festival
Recommended for families. Thousands of multi-colored lights encircle the 225-acre lake with brightly lit displays throughout the Gardens. Annual event.
Hours: 6-10pm
Hodges Gardens & Wilderness *See earlier listing in this section.*
Web: www.hodgespark.com
(318)586-3523

New Orleans

March 14-21
🌿 Gardens of the Mississippi
A river cruise on board the Mississippi Queen starting in New Orleans with stops to see spring gardens in St. Francisville, Natchez, Vicksburg, Greenville and Memphis. For information, call (800)942-6666 or see web site at www.haerttertravel.com.
American Horticultural Society, 7931 East Boulevard Drive, Alexandria, VA 22308
Web: www.ahs.org
(800)777-7931

March 21-25
🌿 New Orleans Home & Garden Show
One of the largest home and garden shows in the southeast with nearly 500 exhibitors. Features 2,000 square feet of show landscapes and garden areas. Annual event, now in its 47th year.
Louisiana Superdome, 1500 Poydras Street, New Orleans, LA
Contact: **Home Builders Association of Greater New Orleans**, 2424 North Arnoult

Be sure to check with the sponsor in advance.

Road, Metairie, LA 70001-1891
Web: www.home-builders.org
(504)837-2700

March 23-24, March 31-April 1
✿ New Orleans Spring Fiesta
A parade of horse-drawn carriages through the French Quarter on the first Saturday of this event and ongoing tours of plantations, private homes and courtyards in and around historic New Orleans. Annual event.
New Orleans Spring Fiesta, 826 St. Ann Street, New Orleans, LA 70116
E-mail: jbcook108@worldnet.att.net
(800)550-8450 or (504)581-1367

April 7-8
✿ Spring Garden Show
Recommended for families. Exhibits by regional nurseries, horticultural businesses, plant societies, landscape companies and government agencies, plus educational gardening lectures, a large plant and garden products sales area and children's activities. Annual event.
Hours: 10am-5pm
Fee: $4; $1 children 5-12; children under 5 free
New Orleans Botanical Garden, City Park, 1 Palm Drive, New Orleans, LA 70124
Web: www.neworleanscitypark.com/garden/
(504)483-9386

October 6-7
✿ Secret Gardens of the French Quarter
Self-guided walking tour of sixteen privately-owned gardens in the historical French

Quarter of New Orleans. Eight different courtyards open each day. Annual event.
Hours: Noon-4pm
Fee: $10 per day
Patio Planters, PO Box 72074, New Orleans, LA 70172
(504)568-9385

October 20-21
✿ Fall Garden Show
Exhibits by regional nurseries, horticultural businesses, plant societies, landscape companies and government agencies, plus educational gardening lectures, a large plant and garden products sales area and children's activities.
New Orleans Botanical Garden *See earlier listing in this section.*
Web: www.neworleanscitypark.com/garden/
(504)483-9386

December
✿ Celebration in the Oaks
Recommended for families. Live oaks decorated with holiday lights along a two-mile stretch in City Park. Contact sponsor for exact dates.
New Orleans Botanical Garden *See earlier listing in this section.*
Web: www.neworleanscitypark.com/garden/
(504)483-9386

December
✿ Celebrate the Season at Longue Vue
Seasonal plant materials throughout the

Remember that schedules do change.

house. Special twilight tours at 4 and 5pm daily. Open until 6pm this month and closed Christmas Day. Annual event. Contact sponsor for exact dates.
Longue Vue House & Gardens, 7 Bamboo Road, New Orleans, LA 70124
Web: www.longuevue.com
(504)488-5488

Saint Francisville

December
🌺 Christmas at Rosedown
A display in the Gardens of ardisia, nandina, holly and the famous camellias at the start of their bloom, plus traditional decorations in the Plantation.
Hours: Every day except Christmas
Fee: Regular admission
Rosedown Plantation & Gardens, 12501 Highway 10, St. Francisville, LA 70775
(225)635-3332

Shreveport

February 17
🌺 Pruning Party
A pruning workshop, followed by the chance to practice on over 22,000 rose bushes in the Gardens. Lunch provided. Interested participants to RSVP the Center and bring gloves and pruners to the party. Annual event. Date tentative. Call to confirm.
Hours: starts 8am
Fee: Free
The Gardens of the American Rose Center, 8877 Jefferson-Paige Road, Shreveport, LA
Mail: **American Rose Society**, PO Box

30,000, Shreveport, LA 71130-0030
Web: www.ars.org
(318)938-5402

April 27 - May 5
🌺 Spring Bloom Festival
A nine-day celebration of the first rose blooms in the Gardens, home to more than 22,000 rose bushes. Garden exhibits, live entertainment and educational seminars. Annual event.
The Gardens of the American Rose Center
See earlier listing in this section.
Web: www.ars.org
(318)938-5402

May 5-6
🌺 Le Tour des Jardins
A self-guided tour of five privately-owned gardens located in Shreveport and Bossier City, Louisiana Garden Bazaar at one of the gardens and refreshments at another. Master Gardeners stationed at all of the gardens to answer questions. Annual event.
Hours: 9am-5pm Sat; noon-5pm Sun
Fee: $10; good for both days
Northwest Louisiana Master Gardeners Association, 419 Regency Blvd, Shreveport, LA 71106
E-mail: docandmem@sprynet.com
(318)797-9977

Late November - December
🌺 Christmas in Roseland
Recommended for families. More than 1,000,000 lights in the gardens, plus model trains, toy soldiers and reindeer. Annual event.

Be sure to check with the sponsor in advance.

The Gardens of the American Rose Center
See earlier listing in this section.
Web: www.ars.org
(318)938-5402

MISSISSIPPI

Biloxi

March 24-25
🌿 **Herb & Garden Fest**
Recommended for families. A festival featuring free lectures, demonstrations, music, children's activities, herb walks, garden tours through private speciality gardens, plus more than seventy vendors offering crafts, plants, food, art, books, garden supplies and healing arts supplies. Free lectures on a variety of topics including identification of herbs, culinary herbs, reflexology, Feng Shui, traditional medical herbalism, cooking, aromatherapy, nutrition, massage therapy, homeopathy, Chinese medicine, iridology, healing touch, Reiki, acupuncture and Ayuvedic medicine. Held in the heart of the oak-lined city of Ocean Springs. Annual event, now in its 8th year.
Hours: 9am-5pm Sat; 10am-4pm Sun
Fee: Most events free
Ocean Springs Chamber of Commerce, 1000 Main Street, Ocean Springs, MS
Contact: **Directions, Inc.**, 4862 Wainwright Cr., Owings Mills, MD 21117
Web: www.herbevent.com
(888)466-2880

Jackson

March 24
🌿 **Spring Celebration & Plant Sale**
Recommended for families. A spring celebration with a plant sale and Q&A with Master Gardeners on Saturday, plus music, clowns and puppet shows for children on Sunday. Refreshments available.
Annual event.
Mynelle Gardens, 4736 Clinton Blvd, Jackson, MS 39209
(601)960-1894

Natchez

March - Mid April
🌿 **Natchez Spring Pilgrimage**
A series of eight tours encompassing 32 historic and private homes and gardens, many of them open only for this tour. Includes morning and afternoon tours, each of which visit four properties. Sponsored by the Home Owners Association.
Annual event.
Natchez Pilgrimage Tours, PO Box 347, Natchez, MS 39121
Web: www.natchezpilgrimage.com
(800)647-6742 or (601)446-6631

October 10-27
🌿 **Fall Pilgrimage**
A series of six tours encompassing 18 historic and private homes and gardens, many of them open only for this tour. Includes morning and afternoon tours, each of which visit three properties. Optional overnights at selected antebellum homes on tour which operate as bed and breakfasts. Sponsored by the Home Owners Association.

Remember that schedules do change.

Annual event.
Fee: $18 per tour; discounts on multiple tours
Natchez Pilgrimage Tours *See earlier listing in this section.*
Web: www.natchezpilgrimage.com
(800)647-6742 or (601)446-6631

Picayune
50 miles from New Orleans

August 18
🌺 Hummingbird Garden Tour
A visit to the private gardens of two noted hummingbird experts. Bring a sack lunch. Car pooling from the Arboretum's visitors parking lot.
The Crosby Arboretum at MSU, 370 Ridge Road, Picayune, MS 39466
Web: www.msstate.edu/dept/crec/camain.html
(601)799-2311

NORTH CAROLINA

Asheville

April
🌺 Festival of Flowers
A spring festival featuring lavish Victorian floral arrangements in Biltmore House, garden strolls and music on the weekends. Timed to coincide with the blooming of the thousands of tulips, iris, flowering dogwoods, Japanese cherry trees and azaleas in the Gardens. Annual event.
Biltmore Estate, Asheville, NC
Mail: 1 North Pack Square, Asheville, NC

28801
Web: www.biltmore.com
(800)543-2961

May 5
🌺 Day in the Gardens
Plant sales, tours of the Gardens, arts and crafts, entertainment and food.
Annual event.
Fee: Free
The Botanical Gardens at Asheville, 151 W.T. Weaver Boulevard, Asheville, NC 28804
(828)252-5190

Barco

March 31 - April 1
🌺 Currituck Flower & Garden Show
A show of indoor theme gardens created by Master Gardeners, plus lectures, educational exhibits and a large market of plants, furniture and garden-related items.
Annual event.
Fee: Free
Currituck County High School, Route 168, Barco, NC
Contact: **Currituck County Master Gardeners**, c/o Extension Office, PO Box 10, Currituck, NC 27929
(252)232-2262

Belmont
West of Charlotte

April 28
🌺 Celebrate Spring! Plant & Craft Sale
Recommended for families. A sale of unique plants and botanical crafts, plus special speakers, interactive children's

activities, music and food. Annual event, now in its 8th year.
Hours: 8:30am-4:30pm
Fee: $4; $2 children 6-12
Daniel Stowe Botanical Garden, 6500 South New Hope Road, Belmont, NC 28012
Web: www.dsbg.org
(704)825-4490

May 28
🌺 Memorial Day Picnic & Concert
A live concert in the Garden. Picnicking permitted.
Fee: $5; children under 13 free
Daniel Stowe Botanical Garden *See earlier listing in this section.*
Web: www.dsbg.org
(704)825-4490

July
🌺 Flutterby, Butterfly
Recommended for families. Includes activities for the whole family, including guided butterfly walks, self-guided tours and slide lectures. Annual event. Contact sponsor for exact date.
Fee: Regular admission
Daniel Stowe Botanical Garden *See earlier listing in this section.*
Web: www.dsbg.org
(704)825-4490

July 4
🌺 Fourth of July Concert & Fireworks
Recommended for families. Patriotic music by the Charlotte Symphony Orchestra in the Garden followed by a fireworks display. Picnicking permitted. Food and beverage vendors available. Annual event, now in its

3rd year.
Hours: Concert 8pm; fireworks 9pm
Fee: $10 per car
Daniel Stowe Botanical Garden *See earlier listing in this section.*
Web: www.dsbg.org
(704)825-4490

August
🌺 Hummingbird Happenings
Demonstrations of the banding of ruby-throated hummingbirds by licensed banders from The Hummer/Bird Study Group, the largest organized hummingbird banding group in the Southeast. Contact sponsor for exact dates.
Fee: Regular admission
Daniel Stowe Botanical Garden *See earlier listing in this section.*
Web: www.dsbg.org
(704)825-4490

August 18
🌺 Balloon Glow
Recommended for families. A display of tethered hot air balloons plus musical entertainment, balloon walks for children, a climbing wall, balloon artists and antique car exhibit. Picnicking permitted and refreshments available. Annual event, now in its 7th year.
Hours: 4-9pm
Fee: $4; $2 for children 12 and under
Daniel Stowe Botanical Garden *See earlier listing in this section.*
Web: www.dsbg.org
(704)825-4490

Remember that schedules do change.

October 6
🌺 **Celebrate Fall! Plant & Craft Sale**
Unusual plants and crafts for sale, plus demonstrations by potters, weavers and beekeepers, special guest lectures, children's activities and musical entertainment.
Hours: 8:30am-4:30pm
Fee: $4, $2 children 6-12
Daniel Stowe Botanical Garden *See earlier listing in this section.*
Web: www.dsbg.org
(704)825-4490

Boone
75 miles from Winston-Salem

May - October
🌺 **Watauga County Farmers' Market**
A High Country weekend market of vegetables, produce, cut flowers, perennials, shrubs, herbs and annuals. A chance to talk with local growers and farmers and buy direct from the source. Includes hard-to-find plants, along with heritage varieties of fruits and vegetables, crafts and home bakery items. Annual event, now in its 27th year.
Hours: May-Oct Sat mornings; also Wed mornings in July-Aug
Fee: Free
Horn-in-the-West Parking Area, Horn in the West Drive, Boone, NC
Contact: **Watauga County Farmers' Market**, PO Box 8, Vilas, NC 28692
E-mail: sggarden@skybest.com
(828)264-2225

July 14
🌺 **Home Garden Tour & Plant Sale**
A tour of unique local homes and gardens,

plus a plant sale at the Gardens.
Annual event.
Daniel Boone Native Gardens, 295 Grover Johnson Raod, Vilas, NC 28692
(828)264-6390

Charlotte

February 24 - March 4
🌺 **Southern Spring Show ★★★**
One of the largest flower and garden shows in the South. An indoor and outdoor exposition featuring dozens of professionally landscaped gardens, a judged flower show, Orchid Pavilion, Bonsai Pavilion, speakers, demonstrations and a large marketplace.
Annual event, now in its 41st year.
Hours: 10am-9pm Sat, Tues-Fri; 10am-6pm Sun, Mon
Fee: $7.50 in advance; $9 at gate; children under 12 free
Charlotte Merchandise Mart, 2500 East Independence Blvd, Charlotte, NC
Contact: **Southern Shows, Inc**, PO Box 36859, Charlotte, NC 28236
Web: www.southernshows.com
(800)849-0248 or (704)376-6594

April 15 - May 15
🌺 **Rhododendron Display**
Natural woodland garden with 4,000 hybrid rhododendrons and native azaleas in spectacular bloom during the month. Over a mile of trails for self-guided walks.
Fee: Free
UNC Charlotte Botanical Gardens, Mary Alexander Road & Craver Road, Charlotte, NC 28223
Mail: **Biology Department, UNCC**, 9201 University City Blvd, Charlotte, NC 28223

Be sure to check with the sponsor in advance.

Web: www.bioweb.uncc.edu/gardens/
(704)687-4055

April 19-20
☙ Plant Sale & Greenhouse Tour
A greenhouse tour featuring hundreds of orchids, a rain forest and carnivorous pitcher plants, plus a sale of common and unusual bedding plants, house plants and native plants.
Hours: 8am-3pm
Fee: Free
UNC Charlotte Botanical Gardens *See earlier listing in this section.*
Web: www.bioweb.uncc.edu/gardens/
(704)687-4055

April 25-28
☙ Wing Haven Spring Plant Sale
A sale of choice bulbs, wildflowers, vines, ground covers, selected Japanese maples and shrubs, including a great selection of antique roses and hydrangeas. Run by the volunteers and benefits the Gardens. Annual event.
Hours: 10am-4pm
Fee: Free
Wing Haven Gardens & Bird Sanctuary, 248 Ridgewood Avenue, Charlotte, NC 28209
E-mail: winghaven@mindspring.com
(704)331-0664

May 12-13
☙ Gardener's Gardens Tour
A tour of Wing Haven Gardens and six private gardens, each of which is tended by owner who is on hand to answer questions and give advice. Benefits the Wing Haven

Foundation. Annual event.
Fee: $20
Wing Haven Gardens & Bird Sanctuary
See earlier listing in this section.
E-mail: winghaven@mindspring.com
(704)331-0664

Mid October
☙ Wing Haven Fall Plant Sale
On sale will be plants that grow well in this region, some propagated at Wing Haven. Run by the volunteers and benefits the Gardens. Annual event. Contact sponsor for exact date.
Hours: 10am-4pm
Fee: Free
Wing Haven Gardens & Bird Sanctuary
See earlier listing in this section.
E-mail: winghaven@mindspring.com
(704)331-0664

October
☙ Wing Haven Symposium
Wing Haven's biennial symposium with nationally-known lecturers and panelists. Contact sponsor for exact date.
Site to be announced, Charlotte, NC
Contact: **Wing Haven Gardens & Bird Sanctuary** *See earlier listing in this section.*
E-mail: winghaven@mindspring.com
(704)331-0664

Fayetteville

May 5
☙ May Day
A festival celebrating spring with a plant sale, food sale, heritage garden demonstrations and children's activities. Annual event.

Remember that schedules do change.

Hours: 10am-2pm
Fee: Free
Cape Fear Botanical Garden, 536 North Eastern Blvd, Fayetteville, NC
Mail: PO Box 53485, Fayetteville, NC 28305
Web: www.capefearbg.org
(910)486-0221

Fletcher

12 miles from Asheville

April 28-29
꧁ Growin' in the Mountains Lawn & Garden Show
A regional show with plant sales, demonstration gardens, talks, many exhibits and vendors.
Hours: 9am-9pm Sat; 10am-5pm Sun
Fee: Free
WNC Agriculture Center, Highway 280 at I-26, Fletcher, NC
Contact: **Blue Ridge Horticulture Association**, 740 Glover Street, Hendersonville, NC 28792
Web: www.brha.org
(828)697-4891

Hickory

June 8-9
꧁ Romance of the Home & Garden Tour
A self-guided tour of local historical homes and gardens. Includes an optional Friday evening hors d'oeuvres and lecture in a lovely garden setting as well as a Saturday box lunch and lecture. Annual event.
Hours: 6-8pm Fri; 9am-6pm Sat
Fee: $25; $35 with box lunch; $50 for both days

Hickory Landmarks Society, PO Box 2341, Hickory, NC 28603
E-mail: hls@abtsnet.net
(828)322-4731

Hillsborough

May 12
꧁ Hillsborough Garden Tour
A tour of ten gardens, three public and seven private, plus a featured speaker at the Old County Courthouse. Speaker this year, Nancy Goodwin, author of several books and owner of Montrose Gardens. Tickets and map available at the Visitor's Center in Hillsborough on day of tour. Annual event.
Hours: Tour 10am-4pm; speaker at 5pm
Hillsborough Garden Club, 2101 Schley Road, Hurdle Mills, NC 27541
E-mail: calaveras@mindspring.com
(919)732-9852

New Bern

March 30-31
꧁ New Bern Spring Historic Homes & Gardens Tours
A tour of approximately twelve historic homes and gardens not usually open to the public, eight churches and other semi-public buildings. Guides at each location. Walk or drive from site to site. Free walking tours of the Tryon Palace Gardens where thousands of tulips are in bloom. Cosponsored by the New Bern Historical Society and the New Bern Preservation Foundation. Annual event.
Hours: 10am-5pm
Fee: $15 in advance; $17.50 day of tour

Be sure to check with the sponsor in advance.

New Bern Preservation Foundation, PO Box 207, New Bern, NC 28563 (252)633-6448

Pinehurst

April 11
🌷 Home & Garden Tour

A self-guided tour of six homes and gardens in the elite Pinehurst, Southern Pines and Horse Country areas. Includes this year a visit to the 300-acre property of the family that developed the exclusive Forest Creek Golf Course. Lunch available at the Country Club of North Carolina where home and garden of an artist is also on view. All proceeds benefit local beautification and special restoration projects. Annual event.
Fee: $18 in advance; $20 day of tour
Southern Pines Garden Club, 145 North Valley Road, Southern Pines, NC 28387 (910)692-1065
Web: www.sandhills.org/tour 2001

Raleigh

May, July, September
🌷 Open Nursery Days

A series of six open weekends at this large production facility which is normally closed to the public. Opportunity to explore four acres of display and trial gardens, five greenhouses, and purchase plants direct from the gardens. Contact sponsor for exact dates.
Hours: 8am-5pm Fri-Sat; 1-5pm Sun
Fee: Free
Juniper Level Gardens, 9241 Sauls Road, Raleigh, NC 27603
Web: www.plantdelights.com
(919)772-4794

May 19
🌷 Raleigh Rose Society Show

A judged show of home-grown roses open to all amateur growers. Annual event, now in its 54th year.
Fee: Free
North Hills Mall, 4217 Six Forks Road (Exit off I-440), Raleigh, NC
Contact: **Raleigh Rose Society**, 8333 South Creek Road, Willow Spring, NC 27592
Web: radicr.home.mindspring.com/home.htm
(919)380-5059

September 8-9
🌷 Gourd Festival

A weekend festival with exhibits of gourds and gourd crafts, demonstrations of how to grow, dry and craft gourds, competitions for growers and crafters. Sponsored by the North Carolina Gourd Society. Annual event, now in its 60th year.
Hours: 9am-5pm
Fee: $3
Site to be announced, Raleigh, NC
Contact: **North Carolina Gourd Society**, 2325 Englewood Avenue, Durham, NC 27705
Web: www.twincreek.com/gourds
(919)286-0494

October
🌷 Rose Garden Tour

A tour of the private rose gardens of society members. Annual event. Contact sponsor for exact date.
Raleigh Rose Society *See earlier listing in this section.*

Remember that schedules do change.

Web: radicr.home.mindspring.com/
home.htm
(919)380-5059

Wilkesboro

55 miles from Winston-Salem

April 26-29
✿ **Merle Fest**
Wildflower tours and a music festival in the
gardens. Annual event.
Fee: Free
Wilkes Community College Gardens,
Wilkesboro, NC
Mail: PO Box 120, Wilkesboro, NC 28697
Web: www.wilkes.cc.nc.us
(336)838-6100

Wilmington

April 5-8
✿ **Azalea Festival**
A community-wide festival celebrating the
blooming of the azaleas. Includes a tour of
private gardens sponsored by the Cape Fear
Garden Club and many other activities
throughout the community. Annual event.
North Carolina Azalea Festival, PO Box 51,
Wilmington, NC 28402
Web: www.azalea.wilmington.org
(910)763-0905

Wilson

May 20
✿ **Sunday in the Rose Garden**
Recommended for families. A public festival
of gardens and art in the Wilson Rose
Garden when its 1000 roses are in full
bloom. Includes "Art in the Rose Garden"

contests for adult and youth artists plus
entertainment and activities for everyone.
This year's feature, dedication of $30,000
Georgia marble sculpture by International
artist Horace Farlowe. Annual event.
Hours: 2-5pm
Fee: Free
Wilson Rose Garden, 1800 Herring
Avenue, Wilson, NC
Mail: PO Box 10, Wilson, NC 27894
Web: www.wilson-nc.com/
wct_rosegarden.html
(800)497-7398

SOUTH CAROLINA

Beaufort

April 28
✿ **Beaufort Garden Walk**
A tour of ten luxurious gardens in historic
Beaufort and surrounding area. Starts at the
Baptist Church. Annual event, now in its 8th
year.
Hours: 10am-5pm
Fee: $20
The Arts Council of Beaufort County, PO
Box 482, Beaufort, SC 29901
E-mail: eric@beaufortarts.com
(843)521-4144

Charleston

February
✿ **Daffodil Days at Magnolia Plantation**
A celebration of spring at America's oldest
continually-planted garden (circa 1680)
with millions of daffodils, flowering fruit

Be sure to check with the sponsor in advance.

trees, early azaleas, full-blooming camellias, spirea, iris, anemones, roses, atamasco lilies and redbud. Tour of Revolutionary Greek Revival Plantation House included. Annual event.
Magnolia Plantation & Gardens, 3550 Ashley River Road, Charleston, SC 29414
Web: www.magnoliaplantation.com
(843)571-1266

March 15 - April 14
Festival of Houses & Gardens ★★★
Tours of private homes and gardens within Charleston's historic district, an area dating back to the 1670s and containing many period buildings. Glorious Gardens guided tours every Thursday. Additional tours to other areas and candlelight tours available. Annual event, now in its 54th year.
Fee: $40 per ticket for each event
Historic Charleston Foundation, 40 East Bay Street, Charleston, SC 29401
Web: www.historiccharleston.org
(843)722-3405

April 7, 14
House & Garden Tours
Tours of private gardens and homes decorated with floral arrangements done by Garden Club members. Refreshments served. Two different tours on two successive Saturdays. Annual event, now in its 66th year.
Hours: 2-5pm
The Garden Club of Charleston, 728 Preservation Place, Charleston, SC 29464
E-mail: bhprcc@aol.com
(843)971-4753

September 20 - October 27
Fall Candlelight Tours of Homes & Gardens
A series of walking tours of historic houses, gardens and churches in Charleston's Historic District on Thursday, Friday and Saturday evenings. Afternoon garden tours and teas on Sundays. Detailed brochure available from the sponsor in August. Annual event.
Hours: 7-10pm Thurs-Sat; 2-5pm Sun
Fee: From $35 per tour
Preservation Society of Charleston, PO Box 521, Charleston, SC 29402
Web: www.preservationsociety.org
(843)722-4630

October 4-7
Charleston Garden Festival
A festival with many major events including a two-day symposium featuring nationally known speakers, tours of the city's finest gardens, horticultural tours of private plantations rarely open to the public, lectures, workshops, a marketplace with over sixty nurseries and garden vendors, indoor show gardens and landscapes, water gardens and floral arrangements. Tickets for the plantation tours, garden tours and lectures sold separately. Proceeds from the show benefit Florence Crittenton Programs, offering shelter, education, medical care and counseling to pregnant women and their children. Many events held at Gaillard Auditorium.
Gaillard Auditorium, 77 Calhoun Street, Charleston, SC
Contact: **Charleston Garden Festival**, 19 St. Margaret Street, Charleston, SC 29403
E-mail: cgf1999@bellsouth.net
(843)722-0661

Remember that schedules do change.

October 14-18
⚜ International Heritage Rose Conference
A convocation of professional and amateur rose gardeners from around the world held in Charleston's historic district with all hotels within walking distance of sessions. Presentations by internationally known speakers on a variety of topics, including the Noisette rose, the first class of rose to be developed. Annual event, now in its 9th year.
College of Charleston, Charleston, SC
Contact: **Charleston Area Convention & Visitors Bureau**, PO Box 975, Charleston, SC 29402
(843)853-8000

December 8
⚜ Holiday Home & Garden Tour
A tour of select historic homes and gardens in downtown Charleston decorated for the holidays using all natural materials. Annual event.
Gibbes Museum of Art, 135 Meeting Street, Charleston, SC 29401
Web: gibbes1@charleston.net
(843)722-2706

Clemson
30 miles from Greenville

Late October
⚜ Fall Celebration
Recommended for families. A celebration of the season with activities for all, including scarecrow making, pumpkin carving, wreath workshops using all natural materials, crafting classes and educational programs. Contact sponsor for exact dates.

The South Carolina Botanical Garden, 102 Garden Trail, Clemson University, Clemson, SC 29634
Web: virtual.clemson.edu/scbg/
(864)656-3405

Columbia

March 29
⚜ SC Midlands Master Gardeners Association Symposium
This year's theme, "The Gardener's Eye." Features Allen Lacy, Jim Long, Pam Baggett, Elizabeth Dean and Jenks Farmer and includes hands-on demonstrations as well as plant and book sales. Annual event, now in its 11th year.
Riverbanks Zoo & Botanical Garden, Columbia, SC
Contact: **SC Midlands Master Gardeners Association**, 1292 Sand Oak Drive, Lugoff, SC 29078
E-mail: grayghos@gateway.net
(803)438-3294

Greenwood

June 22-24
⚜ South Carolina Festival of Flowers
Recommended for families. A popular community-wide festival with many activities, including tours of private gardens, workshops and tours of Park Seed Company's famous trial gardens, a cut flower show, historic home tours, plus a bluegrass festival, arts and crafts, sports and food. Annual event, now in its 34th year.
Fee: Free for most events
South Carolina Festival of Flowers, PO Box 980, Greenwood, SC 29648

Be sure to check with the sponsor in advance.

Web: www.scfestivalofflowers.org
(864)223-8411

Hilton Head

May 19
**⚘ All Saints Episcopal Church
Garden Tour**
A tour of ten private gardens on Hilton Head Island and across the bridge in Bluffton. Picnic lunch available at the Church Parish Hall, plus a bake shop and sale of herbs and plants. Annual event.
Hours: 10am; lunch 11am-2pm
Fee: $15; $20 with lunch
All Saints Episcopal Church, 3001 Meeting Street, Hilton Head, SC 29926
E-mail: hhsaints@aol.com
(843)681-8333

Orangeburg

45 miles from Columbia

April 27-29
⚘ South Carolina Festival of Roses
Recommended for families. A festival in the Edisto Memorial Gardens, timed to coincide with the beginning of the rose blooming season. Includes live entertainment, sports tournaments, races, arts and crafts, plus a display of at least seventy-five varieties of roses in this official All-America Rose Selection test garden. Annual event, now in its 45th year.
Hours: 1-5pm Fri; 9am-6pm Sat; 1-5pm Sun
Fee: Free
Edisto Memorial Gardens, Highway 301 South, Orangeburg, SC
Contact: **Orangeburg County Chamber of Commerce**, PO Box 328, Orangeburg, SC

29116-0328
Web: www.orangeburgsc.net
(803)534-6821

Sumter

May 5
⚘ Secret Backyard Tour & Garden Picnic
A tour through the gardens of Sumter's historic homes, plus a garden picnic or tea. Sponsored by the Council of Garden Clubs in Sumter. Annual event.
Hours: 10am-4pm
Fee: $15
Sumter Convention & Visitors Bureau, 32 East Calhoun Street, Sumter, SC 29150
Web: www.irisfestival.org
(800)688-4748

May 24-27
⚘ Iris Festival ★★★
Recommended for families. A community-wide festival celebrating the blooming of Swan Lake Iris Gardens, one of the world's most spectacular array of Japanese irises. Over 6,000,000 plants in bloom on 150 acres along the banks of the Lake, home to the eight known species of swans. Includes a parade, garden shows, arts, crafts, entertainment and children's activities. Named one of the top 100 events in North America by the American Bus Association and one of the top 20 by the Southeastern Tourism Association. Annual event.
Hours: 6:30-9pm Thurs; 8am-9pm Fri-Sat; 1-6pm Sun
Fee: Free
Liberty Street, Sumter, SC
Contact: **Sumter Convention & Visitors Bureau** *See earlier listing in this section.*

Remember that schedules do change.

Web: www.irisfestival.org
(800)688-4748

TENNESSEE

Chattanooga

April 2-8
❧ **Wildflower Celebration**
A week of educational workshops followed by naturalist-led trail tours of the wildflowers on Saturday and Sunday. Includes excursions by canoe, mountain bike and horseback as well as walking tours. Sponsored by the Tennessee Wildflower Society, Tennessee Aquarium and the North Chickamauga Creek Conservatory. Annual event.
Tennessee Aquarium, One Broad Street, Chattanooga, TN
Mail: PO Box 11048, Chattanooga, TN 37401
E-mail: ecn@tennis.org
(423)785-4071

April 13-15
❧ **Spring Wildflower Festival & Native Plant Sale**
Guided wildflower walks, mini stump talks and a sale of hundreds of varieties of native trees, shrubs and wildflowers, most of them propagated at Reflection Riding. Annual event.
Fee: Free entry to this event
Reflection Riding Arboretum & Botanical Garden, 400 Garden Road, Chattanooga, TN 37419
Web: virtual.chattanooga.net/ rriding
(423)821-9582

Gatlinburg

April 26-28
❧ **Spring Wildflower Pilgrimage**
Over 100 guided walks to see the wildflowers, birds and other wildlife in the Great Smokies, all led by subject-matter experts. Attracts 1500 visitors a year. Register at the W.L. Mills Auditorium in Gatlinburg.
Great Smoky Mountains National Park, 107 Park Headquarters Road, Gatlinburg, TN 37738
Web: GRSMSmokiesinformation@nps.gov
(423)436-1218 or (423)436-1224

Jackson

February 23-25
❧ **West Tennessee Lawn & Garden Show**
A regional show featuring indoor show gardens, fifty exhibitors, education booths and three days of seminars presented by the Master Gardeners.
Hours: noon-8pm Fri; 8am-8pm Sat; noon-5pm Sun
Fairgrounds Park, Highway 45 S, Jackson, TN
Contact: **West Tennessee Lawn & Garden Show**, 1061 Highway 45 Bypass, Jackson, TN 38301
(901)664-6161

Knoxville

February 22-25
❧ **Dogwood Arts Festival House & Garden Show**
Features beautiful blooming show gardens, workshops led by HGTV experts and more than 275 exhibitors of products and services for home and garden. Annual event,

Be sure to check with the sponsor in advance.

now in its 23rd year.
Hours: 4-9pm Thurs; 10am-9pm Fri-Sat;
noon-6pm Sun
Fee: $7; discounts for seniors and students;
children under 12 free
Knoxville Convention & Exhibition Center,
Knoxville, TN
Contact: **Dogwood Arts Festival**, 111 North
Central Avenue, Knoxville, TN 37902
(865)637-4561 or (800)DOGWOOD

April 6-29
❦ **Dogwood Arts Festival**
Recommended for families. A festival celebrating the blooming of the dogwoods with
more than 60 miles of dogwood trails, over
100 open gardens and more than forty
events throughout Knoxville, ranging from a
flower show by area clubs to arts and crafts
on Market Square Mall, art, photography
and quilting exhibitions. Annual event, now
in its 41st year.
Dogwood Arts Festival *See earlier listing in
this section.*
(865)637-4561 or (800)DOGWOOD

Mid May
❦ **Secret Gardens Tour**
A tour of private gardens in the Knoxville
area to benefit the Gardens at the University
of Tennessee, Knoxville. Includes five pri-
vate gardens and the University of
Tennessee Institute of Agriculture Gardens
on Neyland Drive. Annual event. Contact
sponsor for exact date.
Hours: 1-6pm
Fee: $15
**Friends of Gardens at University of
Tennessee**, PO Box 51394, Knoxville,

TN 37950
Web: www.korrnet.org/gardens/
(865)525-4555

Memphis

March 9-11
❦ **Kiwanis Garden Expo**
A exhibition by landscapers, nurserymen,
florists, growers, interior designers, crafts-
men, artisans and vendors from all over the
country. Features showcase walk-through
innovative landscaped garden displays.
Sponsored by the Cordova Kiwanis
Foundation, Inc. and all profits benefit chil-
dren's charities. Annual event.
Hours: 10am-8pm Fri; 10am-6pm Sat;
10am-5pm Sun
Fee: $5; children under 12 free
Agricenter International, Walnut Grove
Road & Germantown Parkway,
Memphis, TN
Contact: **Kiwanis Garden Expo**, 7777
Walnut Grove Road, Box 14, Memphis,
TN 38120
Web: www.gardenexpo.org
(901)757-8788

April 8
❦ **Open Day at the Wild Flower Garden**
Open day at one of the Garden's most spe-
cial areas with guided tours by members of
the Wild Flower Society of Memphis.
Annual event.
Memphis Botanic Garden, 750 Cherry
Road, Memphis, TN 38117
Web: www.memphisbotanicgarden.com
(901)685-1566

Remember that schedules do change.

April 13-15
🌿 Spring's Best Plant Sale
Thousands of plants especially tested to grow well in the region including perennials, annuals, vines, hostas, scented geraniums, salvia, ferns, wildflowers, roses, trees, country garden plants and garden accessories. One of the largest plant sales in the mid-South. Annual event, now in its 26th year. Date tentative. Call to confirm.
Fee: Free admission to Garden during sale hours
Memphis Botanic Garden *See earlier listing in this section.*
Web: www.memphisbotanicgarden.com
(901)685-1566

May 13
🌿 Memphis Rose Society Mother's Day Show
A show that draws competitors from a four-state area and a sale of miniature and cut roses. Rose culture information available. Annual event.
Hours: Judging 10am-noon; open to public 1-5pm
Fee: Free
Oak Court Mall, Poplar Avenue at Perkins, Memphis, TN
Contact: **Memphis Rose Society**, 2676 Juneway, Memphis, TN 38134
E-mail: dalericson@aol.com
(662)890-6106

May 13
🌿 Mother's Day in the Garden
Live music, lunch in the Japanese Garden and a complimentary flower for Mom. Horse drawn carriage rides through the Garden for

an additional fee. Annual event.
Memphis Botanic Garden *See earlier listing in this section.*
Web: www.memphisbotanicgarden.com
(901)685-1566

September 22
🌿 Herb Symposium
A day-long symposium on herbs sponsored by the Memphis Herb Society.
Annual event.
Memphis Botanic Garden *See earlier listing in this section.*
Web: www.memphisbotanicgarden.com
(901)685-1566

September 29-30
🌿 Japanese Festival
A festival celebrating Japanese art and culture. Includes Bonsai and Ikebana demonstrations, calligraphy, kendo origami, live Japanese music, ethnic food and candlelight tours of the Japanese Garden of Tranquility.
Memphis Botanic Garden *See earlier listing in this section.*
Web: www.memphisbotanicgarden.com
(901)685-1566

October 7
🌿 Dixie Rose Club Fall Show
A judged competition of roses in seventy-two classifications and rose arrangements in eleven categories, plus a sale of rose blooms and miniature rose plants. Rose culture information available. Annual event.
Hours: 1-5pm
Fee: Free
Memphis Botanic Garden, 750 Cherry

Be sure to check with the sponsor in advance.

Road, Memphis, TN
Contact: **Dixie Rose Club**, 2729 Sage
Meadow Drive, Memphis, TN 38133
E-mail: dalericson@aol.com
(662)890-6106

October 28
☙ Old-Fashioned Harvest Festival
Recommended for families. Exhibits in celebration of harvest time and activities for the
whole family. Annual event. Date tentative.
Call to confirm.
Memphis Botanic Garden *See earlier listing in this section.*
Web: www.memphisbotanicgarden.com
(901)685-1566

Nashville

February 8-11
☙ The Antiques & Garden Show of
Nashville ★★★
Features full-scale display gardens and
striking exhibits that blend antiques, decorative arts and floral design. Featured
speakers this year, HRH Princess Michael of
Kent, Martha Stewart and Bunny Williams.
Named by the Southeastern Tourism
Society as one of the top twenty events in
the Southeast. Benefits The Exchange Club
of Nashville Charities, Inc. and Cheekwood
Museum and Botanical Gardens. Annual
event, now in its 11th year.
Hours: 10am-8pm Thurs-Fri; 10am-7pm
Sat; 11am-5pm Sun
Fee: $10 in advance; $12 at gate; $9
seniors; children under 12 free; lecture tick-
ets sold separately
Nashville Convention Center, Nashville, TN
Contact: **Antiques & Garden Show of**

Nashville, PO Box 50950, 1200 Forrest
Park Drive, Nashville, TN 37205
Web: www.antiques&gardenshow.com
(615)352-1282

February 24-25
☙ Camellia Show
A show staged by the Middle Tennessee
Camellia Society featuring hundreds of
blooms by exhibitors from several states
with experts on hand to answer questions.
Annual event.
Hours: 9:30am-4:30pm Sat; 11am-
4:30pm Sun
Fee: Regular admission
Cheekwood Botanical Garden, 1200
Forrest Park Drive, Nashville, TN 37205
Web: www.cheekwood.org
(615)356-8000

March 1-4
☙ Nashville Lawn & Garden Show
This year's theme, "2001: A Plant Odyssey."
Features a one-acre display of live gardens,
free series of educational lectures, 250
exhibit booths and a floral gallery with displays by floral designers. Regional show
presented by the Horticultural Association
of Tennessee.
Hours: 10am-9pm Thurs-Sat;
10am-5pm Sun
Fee: $7; $6 seniors; $1 children 12
and under
Tennessee State Fairgrounds, Exit
Wedgewood Avenue off I-65, Nashville, TN
Contact: **Nashville Lawn & Garden Show**,
5711 Old Harding Road, Suite 6, Nashville,
TN 37205
(615)352-3863

Remember that schedules do change.

March 31 - April 1
🌿 **Wildflower Fair**
A celebration of native wildflowers featuring a sale of hundreds of native plants and tours of Cheekwood's wildflower garden at the height of its spring bloom. Sponsored by the Garden Club of Nashville. Annual event.
Hours: 9:30am-4:30pm Sat; 11am-4:30pm Sun
Fee: Regular admission
Cheekwood Botanical Garden *See earlier listing in this section.*
Web: www.cheekwood.org
(615)356-8000

March 31 - April 1
🌿 **Daffodil Show**
A show of many of the best daffodil varieties in the region, sponsored by the Daffodil Society of Middle Tennessee. Annual event.
Hours: 1-4:30pm Sat; 11am-4:30pm Sun
Fee: Regular admission
Cheekwood Botanical Garden *See earlier listing in this section.*
Web: www.cheekwood.org
(615)356-8000

April 21-22
🌿 **Bonsai Show & Sale**
A display of finished, show-quality specimens, some over 100 years old, as well as unfinished, training examples of this ancient art form. Includes a sale of bonsai plants and tools and demonstrations by members of the Nashville Bonsai Society. Annual event.
Hours: 9:30am-4:30pm Sat; 11am-4:30pm Sun

Fee: Regular admission
Cheekwood Botanical Garden *See earlier listing in this section.*
Web: www.cheekwood.org
(615)356-8000

May 11-12
🌿 **Community Flower Show**
Showcases floral arrangements and horticulture entries by members of area garden clubs. Presented by the Horticultural Society of Middle Tennessee. Annual event.
Hours: 1-4:30pm Fri; 9:30am-4:30pm Sat
Fee: Regular admission
Cheekwood Botanical Garden *See earlier listing in this section.*
Web: www.cheekwood.org
(615)356-8000

May 26-27
🌿 **Rose Show**
A show that draws exhibitors from a number of states presented by the Rose Society of Nashville. Includes a sale of roses. Annual event. Date tentative. Call to confirm.
Hours: 9:30am-4:30pm Sat; 11am-4:30pm Sun
Fee: $10; $8 seniors; $5 youth (6-17) & college students
Cheekwood Botanical Garden *See earlier listing in this section.*
Web: www.cheekwood.org
(615)356-8000

June 2-3
🌿 **Hosta Show**
A cut-leaf show of hostas presented by the Middle Tennessee Hosta Society, displaying a wide variety of leaf forms, sizes and variegation. Annual event, now in its 2nd year.

Be sure to check with the sponsor in advance.

Hours: 9:30am-4:30pm Sat;
11am-4:30pm Sun
Fee: Regular admission
Cheekwood Botanical Garden *See earlier*
listing in this section.
Web: www.cheekwood.org
(615)356-8000

June 23
✿ Daylily Show & Sale
A flower show for daylily lovers. Includes a
sale of daylilies by members of the Middle
Tennessee Daylily Society. Annual event.
Hours: Sale 10am-2pm; show 12:30-
4:30pm
Fee: Regular admission
Cheekwood Botanical Garden *See earlier*
listing in this section.
Web: www.cheekwood.org
(615)356-8000

September 22-23
✿ Gesneriad Show
A judged show with horticultural entries,
flower arrangements and a plant sale.
Sponsored by the Tennessee Gesneriad
Society. Annual event.
Hours: 9:30am-4:30pm Sat; 11am-
4:30pm Sun
Fee: Regular admission
Cheekwood Botanical Garden *See earlier*
listing in this section.
Web: www.cheekwood.org
(615)356-8000

October 5-6
✿ Perennials Conference
A day-long conference on Saturday with
presentations by noted authors and lecturers. Optional tours of the Cheekwood gar-

dens on Friday and a reception on Friday
evening. Presented by Cheekwood and the
Perennial Plant Society of Middle
Tennessee. Annual event, now in its
12th year.
Hours: 9:30-4:30 Sat
Cheekwood Botanical Garden *See earlier*
listing in this section.
Web: www.cheekwood.org
(615)356-8000

October 20-21
✿ Orchid Show
A large show with displays by orchid societies and vendors from several states presented by the Orchid Society of Middle
Tennessee. Includes a sale of a wide variety
of orchids. Annual event.
Hours: 9:30am-4:30pm Sat; 11am-
4:30pm Sun
Fee: Regular admission
Cheekwood Botanical Garden *See earlier*
listing in this section.
Web: www.cheekwood.org
(615)356-8000

November 23 - December 27
✿ Trees of Christmas
Recommended for families. Seasonal dis-
play of holiday trees sponsored by the
Horticultural Society of Middle Tennessee.
Annual event.
Hours: 9:30am-4:30pm Mon-Sat; 11am-
4:30pm Sun
Fee: Regular admission
Cheekwood Botanical Garden *See earlier*
listing in this section.
Web: www.cheekwood.org
(615)356-8000

Remember that schedules do change.

Oak Ridge

May 4-6
⚘ Arboretum Plant Sale
A sale known by astute horticulturists for its rare, new and improved cultivars, plus information for beginning gardeners. Annual event, now in its 36th year.
Hours: Member's preview 5-7pm Fri; open to public 9am-4pm Sat, noon-4pm Sun
Fee: Free
University of Tennessee Arboretum, 901 Kerr Hollow Road (Route 62), Oak Ridge, TN
Contact: **University of Tennessee Arboretum Society**, PO Box 5382, Oak Ridge, TN 37831
Web: www.kornet.org/utas/
(865)483-4843

Roan Mountain

June
⚘ Rhododendron Festival
A celebration of the largest natural display of Catawba rhododendron in the world growing at the top of Roan Mountain, 6,285 feet above sea level. Features tours, arts and crafts, music and old time events to celebrate the blooming of the rhododendrons. Annual event. Contact sponsor for exact date.
Hours: 8am-5pm
Fee: Free
Roan Mountain State Park, Roan Mountain, TN
Contact: **Rhododendron Fest, Roan Mountain**, Chamber of Commerce, PO 190, Elizabethton, TN 37643
(423)772-0190 or (423)547-3852

VIRGIN ISLANDS

Frederiksted

July
⚘ Mango Melee
Mango workshops, food, drinks, vendors of mango products, arts and crafts, plus a huge nursery sale. Annual event. Contact sponsor for exact date.
St. George Village Botanical Garden, 127 Estate St. George, Frederiksted, VI 00840
E-mail: pcharles@viaccess.net
(340)692-2874

VIRGINIA

Statewide

April 21-28
⚘ Historic Garden Week in Virginia ★★★
Showcases more than 250 of the state's most outstanding homes, gardens and historic landmarks. Three dozen tours scheduled on different days of the week throughout the state. Detailed guidebook available in February from the sponsor for a $5 donation to Historic Garden Week. Tickets can be obtained on day of tour at each garden or at the local tour center. Call or visit the web site for more information. Sponsored by The Garden Club of Virginia and its local garden clubs. Proceeds fund grounds and gardens restorations of Historic Landmarks in Virginia.
Hours: 10am-5pm unless otherwise noted in guidebook
Fee: $15-$25 per tour
Historic Garden Week Headquarters, 12

Be sure to check with the sponsor in advance.

East Franklin Street, Richmond, VA 23219
Web: www.VAGardenweek.org
(804)644-7776

Abingdon

April 27-29
⚜ **Historic Abingdon Garden Faire**
One of the South's most widely acclaimed
country garden shows. Includes a popular
Garden Marketplace featuring an enormous
variety of garden-related merchandise, a
Tea Garden, lectures, children's activities,
helpful demonstrations and special
presentations.
Hours: 10am-6pm Fri-Sat; 11am-5pm Sun
Fee: $4; children under 12 free
**Southwest Virginia Higher Education
Center**, Interstate 81 exit 14, Jonesboro
Road, Abingdon, VA
Contact: **Washington County Virginia
Master Gardeners**, 234 West Valley Street,
Abingdon, VA 24210
Web: www.abingdon.com
(540)676-6309

Alexandria

May 19
⚜ **Spring Garden Day**
A sale by vendors and plant societies of
wildflowers, azaleas, rare and unusual
perennials and shrubs, house plants, herbs
and garden accessories. Annual event.
Hours: 10am-3pm
Fee: Free
Green Spring Gardens, 4603 Green
Springs Road, Alexandria, VA 22312
Web: www.greenspring.org
(703)642-5173

September 22
⚜ **Fall Garden Day**
A sale by Friends of Green Spring, various
plant societies and vendors of rare and
unusual plants, native plants, mums,
orchids, choice perennials, cacti and
other plants.
Hours: 10am-3pm
Green Spring Gardens *See earlier listing in
this section.*
Web: www.greenspring.org
(703)642-5173

Boyce
9 miles east of Winchester

May 12-13
⚜ **Garden Fair**
Recommended for families. An enormous
array of woody and herbaceous plant mate-
rial for sale, plus gardening supplies, seeds
and books. Includes free tours of the Native
Plant Trail, the curator's Spring tour of the
Arboretum, garden lectures and educational
programs for children. One of Northern
Virginia's largest horticultural events.
Sponsored by the Foundation of the State
Arboretum of Virginia. Annual event, now in
its 13th year.
Hours: 10am-4pm
Fee: Parking fee
State Arboretum of Virginia, 400 Blandy
Farm Lane, Boyce, VA 22620
Web: www.virginia.edu/~blandy/home.html
(540)837-1758

October 7
⚜ **Arborfest**
Recommended for families. A celebration of
Arbor Day focusing on different aspects of

Remember that schedules do change.

arborculture and horticulture. Free guided tours of the ginkgos and maples, lots of demonstrations, lectures, food and activities for everyone. Annual event.
Hours: Noon-4:30pm
Fee: Donation requested
State Arboretum of Virginia *See earlier listing in this section.*
Web: www.virginia.edu/~blandy/home.html
(540)837-1758

Chantilly
Near Washington, DC

February 23-25
�花 **Capital Home & Garden Show**
A large regional show of home and garden products and services. Features show gardens and seminars on home remodeling, decorating and gardening. Annual event.
Capital Expo Center, Chantilly, VA
Contact: **dmg world media, Inc.**, 325 Essjay Road, Suite100, Williamsville, NY 14221
(800)274-6948

Charlottesville

April 24-25
�花 **Historic Garden Week at Ashlawn Highland**
Tours of the house and gardens of Ashlawn Highland, the home of President James Monroe. Part of a state-wide celebration of Historic Garden Week. Annual event.
Ashlawn Highland, Home of James Monroe, 1000 James Monroe Parkway, Charlottesville, VA 22902
Web: www.monticello.avenue.org/ashlawn/
(804)293-9539

May - October
�花 **Escorted Garden Tours**
The second Sunday of each month, tours of the gardens led by staff Master Gardeners, followed by beverages and Q&A sessions.
Hours: 2pm
Fee: Regular Admission
Ashlawn Highland, Home of James Monroe *See earlier listing in this section.*
Web: www.monticello.avenue.org/ashlawn/
(804)293-9539

Fredericksburg

February - November
🌺 **First Saturdays in the Gardens**
A series of educational sessions, workshops and walks held the first Saturday of each month at a different historic venue. Venues include Belmont, Kenmore, Chatham Manor, Mary Washington House and other locations. Sponsored by the Master Gardeners in conjunction with the Virginia Cooperative Extension Service and the various historic sites.
Master Gardeners of Rappahannock Area, Stafford County Extension, 405 Chatham Square Office Park, Fredericksburg, VA 22405
Web: www.ext.bt.edu
(540)899-4020

Gloucester
30 miles from Newport News

April 7
🌺 **Daffodil Festival**
Recommended for families. A Main Street family festival featuring entertainment, the daffodil show by the Garden Club of

Be sure to check with the sponsor in advance.

Gloucester, parade, fine art show, original hand craft show, bulb sales, storytellers, historic displays, food, children's games and rides. Shuttle parking available at Gloucester High School. Bus tours available to Brent and Becky's Bulbs for guided tours featuring new hybrids of daffodils and tulips. Annual event, now in its 15th year.
Hours: 9am-4:30pm
Fee: Free; bus tours $4
Main Street, Gloucester, VA
Contact: **Daffodil Festival Committee & Gloucester Parks & Recreation**, PO Box 157, Gloucester, VA 23061
Web: www.co.gloucester.va.us
(804)693-2355

Leesburg

30 miles west of Washington, DC

Late April
🌺 Leesburg Flower & Garden Festival
Recommended for families. Transforms historic downtown Leesburg into a botanical garden. A festival with landscape displays, retail booths, guided walking tours of historic downtown Leesburg, musical entertainment, food, drink and children's activities. Annual event. Contact sponsor for exact dates.
Hours: 10am-6pm Sat; 10am-5pm Sun
Fee: $3; $2 seniors & children; children under 7 free
Historic Downtown Leesburg, King & Market Streets, Leesburg, VA
Contact: **Leesburg Flower & Garden Festival**, 50 Ida Lee Drive NW, Leesburg, VA 20176
Web: www.parksandrec.lessburgva.org
(703)777-1368

May 5
🌺 Goose Creek Herb Fair
Recommended for families. Free herb related demonstrations and lectures, plus fresh baked herbal breads and vendors with a variety of herbs, perennials, flowers, roses, herbal products and crafts for sale. Catered light herbal lunch, music and children's activity area. Annual event, now in its 21st year.
Hours: 10am-4pm
Fee: Free entry to Fair; fee for Oatlands mansion tour
Oatlands Plantation, Route 15, 6 miles south of town, Leesburg, VA
Contact: **Goose Creek Herb Guild**, PO Box 2224, Leesburg, VA 20177
Web: www.herbsearch.com
(703)450-4574

Lynchburg

May 12
🌺 Rose Festival
Garden walks and talks by Cemetery rosarian Thelma Chow at peak bloom time of more than 200 varieties of antique roses along the old brick wall and in the Carl Cato Garden. Plus a sale of antique rose varieties at the Cemetery Center. Annual event, now in its 6th year.
Hours: 10am-3pm
Fee: Free
Old City Cemetery, Directions available at Lynchburg Visitors Center, 12th & Church Streets, Lynchburg, VA
Contact: **Southern Memorial Association**, 401 Taylor Street, Lynchburg, VA 24501
Web: www.gravegarden.org
(804)847-1465

Remember that schedules do change.

Manassas
40 minutes west of DC on I-66

May 26
🌹 Old Rose Celebration
A celebration of old garden roses featuring guided garden tours, local and regional horticultural exhibits, a plant sale and auction of potted old roses. Annual event, now in its 5th year.
Fee: Free
The Old Rose Garden at Ben Lomond Manor House, 10311 Sudley Manor Drive, Manassas, VA
Mail: **Ben Lomond Community Center**, 10501 Copeland Drive, Manassas, VA 20109
Web: www.geocities.com/~oldrosegarden/ (703)369-6925 or (703)368-8784

Middleburg
45 minutes from Washington, DC

May 19-20
🌹 Middleburg Garden Tour
A self-guided driving tour of private estates in the heart of Virginia horse country, plus a market with two dozen vendors in the center of Middleburg. Tickets available by calling or writing the Loudoun Tourism Council or visiting the Council office at 108-D Street (Market Station). Annual event, now in its 9th year.
Hours: 11am-5pm rain or shine
Fee: $20 in advance; $25 day of tour; children 12 and under free
Loudoun Tourism Council, PO Box 1534, Middleburg, VA 20118
(800)752-6118

Mount Vernon

April 21 - May 6
🌹 Gardening Days at Mount Vernon
Recommended for families. An outdoor plant, gift and garden sale near George Washington's historic upper garden, when the magnificent formal and vegetable gardens are at their best. Includes guided tours of the landscape and gardens as well as children's activities and historic gardening demonstrations. Annual event.
Hours: 9:30am-5pm rain or shine
Fee: Regular admission
George Washington's Mount Vernon, South end of GW Memorial Parkway, Mount Vernon, VA
Mail: PO Box 110, Mount Vernon, VA 22121
Web: www.mountvernon.org
(703)780-2000

September 8-9
🌹 The 18th Century Fair at Mount Vernon
Recommended for families. A colonial fair featuring over 60 crafts people selling traditional wares such as basketry, woodcarving, iron work and weavings, plus demonstrations by colonial-attired artisans, colonial-style music, free sightseeing cruises aboard the Potomac Spirit, 18th-century entertainment and refreshments. Annual event.
Hours: 9am-5pm
George Washington's Mount Vernon *See earlier listing in this section.*
Web: www.mountvernon.org
(703)780-2000

Be sure to check with the sponsor in advance.

October 27-28

🌿 Fall Harvest Family Days

Recommended for families. A harvest celebration featuring a chance to meet "General Washington," wheat treading and farrier (blacksmithing) demonstrations, hands-on activities for all ages, wagon rides, a bake sale and discounted cruises aboard the Potomac Spirit. Held at the George Washington: Pioneer Farmer site following harvest of the crops. Annual event.

Hours: 9am-5pm

Fee: $20 family of 4; $3 per person for cruise

George Washington's Mount Vernon *See earlier listing in this section.*

Web: www.mountvernon.org

(703)780-2000

New Castle

October 13

🌿 Craig County Fall Festival

Activities on Main Street in New Castle, including crafts, homemade breads, jams and jellies, tours of the Old Brick Hotel. A good time to walk the Fenwick Mines Wetlands Trail maintained by the New Castle Garden Club. Sponsored by the Craig County Historical Society. Annual event.

Hours: 8am-5:30pm

Fee: Free

New Castle Garden Club, 3856 Carvins Cove Road, Salem, VA 24153

(540)384-7226

Norfolk

April 19

🌿 Southern Living Gardening School

Three classes on gardening topics conducted by expert instructors from Southern Living's Gardening School.

Hours: 8am-3pm

Fee: Fee charged

Norfolk Botanical Garden, 6700 Azalea Garden Road, Norfolk, VA 23518

Web: www.virginiagarden.org

(757)441-5830

May 3-6

🌿 Birds & Blossoms Festival

Recommended for families. A festival celebrating spring and the abundant wildlife of the region. Includes sunrise hikes, garden, bird and butterfly tours, water fowl boat tours, clinics and lectures, games, crafts and a vendor marketplace. Also satellite tours to other state parks and refuges. Sponsored by the Garden in conjunction with the Virginia Department of Game and Inland Fisheries. First year for this event.

Hours: 6am-4pm

Fee: Fee charged

Norfolk Botanical Garden *See earlier listing in this section.*

Web: www.virginiagarden.org

(757)441-5830

May 11-13

🌿 Spring Gardener's Market

A large market with more than twenty-five vendors of plants, garden accessories and wildlife supplies. Free admission to the Garden on these days. Annual event.

Hours: 9am-6pm Fri-Sat; 9am-4pm Sun

Fee: Free

Norfolk Botanical Garden *See earlier listing in this section.*

Web: www.virginiagarden.org

Remember that schedules do change.

(757)441-5830

October 5-7
🪴 History Alive!
Recommended for families. More than fifteen reenactments of historical events, ranging from the medieval period through the present. Includes field maneuvers, battle and sailing scenes by actors in period dress and narrators that explain the action. Also a vendor's marketplace with garden accessories and interesting memorabilia for sale. Annual event.
Hours: 9am-4pm
Fee: Regular admission
Norfolk Botanical Garden *See earlier listing in this section.*
Web: www.virginiagarden.org
(757)441-5830

Thanksgiving - New Year's
🪴 Garden of Lights
Recommended for families. A celebration of the season with thousands of lights in the Garden. Annual event.
Norfolk Botanical Garden *See earlier listing in this section.*
Web: www.virginiagarden.org
(757)441-5830

Richmond

February 22-25
🪴 Maymont Flower & Garden Show ★★★
On of the Southeast's largest flower and garden shows. Features full-size demonstration gardens by talented designers, a top-notch speaker series and a large marketplace of garden-related merchandise.

Recently named one of the American Bus Association's "Top 100 Events in North America."
Hours: 9am-8pm Thurs-Sat; 9am-6pm Sun
Fee: $10 in advance; $12 at door
Richmond Centre, 400 East Marshall Street, Richmond, VA
Contact: **Maymont Foundation**, 1700 Hampton Street, Richmond, VA 23220
Web: www.maymont.org
(804)358-7166

March 31 - April 1
🪴 Lewis Ginter Botanical Garden Daffodil Show
A judged show presented by the Virginia Daffodil Society. Held at the height of the daffodil bloom in the Lucy Payne Minor Memorial Garden. Annual event.
Lewis Ginter Botanical Garden, 1800 Lakeside Avenue, Richmond, VA 23228
Web: www.lewisginter.org
(804)262-9887

April 13-14
🪴 Spring Garden Fair & Plant Sale
A sale of seasonal and unusual plants by more than three dozen vendors.
Lewis Ginter Botanical Garden *See earlier listing in this section.*

April 28
🪴 Maymont's Herbs Galore
A popular festival centered around Maymont's celebrated Herb Garden. Includes cooking demonstrations, garden walks, seminars and a marketplace on the Carriage House lawn, featuring more than forty plant and craft vendors. Annual event,

Be sure to check with the sponsor in advance.

now in its 17th year.
Hours: 9am-5pm
Fee: Free admission; seminar fees vary and early registration recommended
Maymont, 2201 Shields Lake Drive, Richmond, VA
Mail: **Maymont Foundation**, 1700 Hampton Street, Richmond, VA 23220
Web: www.maymont.org
(804)358-7166

May 3 - June 14
🌺 Groovin' in the Garden
Live music on Thursday evenings in the Garden. Annual event.
Hours: 6:30-9:30pm Thurs only
Fee: $10 in advance; $12 day of show
Lewis Ginter Botanical Garden *See earlier listing in this section.*
Web: www.lewisginter.org
(804)262-9887

September 14-15
🌺 Fall Garden Fair & Plant Sale
Seasonal and unique plants for sale by more than forty vendors.
Hours: 9am-5pm Fri; 9am-3pm Sat
Fee: Sale is free; regular admission to Garden
Lewis Ginter Botanical Garden *See earlier listing in this section.*

December
🌺 Gardenfest of Lights
Recommended for families. A holiday tradition with outdoor colorful light displays and beautiful botanical holiday decorations. Annual event.
Lewis Ginter Botanical Garden *See earlier listing in this section.*

Roanoke

June 9-10
🌺 Blue Ridge Garden Festival
Recommended for families. A festival with prominent speakers, demonstrations, lush display gardens created by area nurseries, a vendor marketplace of garden-related merchandise, food and children's activities. Held at the Park, an 1,100-acre outdoor living history museum and nature center. Annual event. Dates tentative. Call to confirm.
Virginia's Explore Park, Milepost 115, Blue Ridge Pkwy, Roanoke, VA
Mail: PO Box 8508, Roanoke, VA 24014
Web: www.explorepark.com/gardenfest
(540)427-1800

Stafford County
55 miles from Washington, DC

May 5
🌺 Family Garden Festival
Recommended for families. A festival with exhibits, vendors, tours, games and other children's activities, held this year in a new venue while Kenmore mansion is undergoing restoration. Also scheduled at this time, archeological displays from current on-site digs and the dedication ceremony of the new Children's Garden at Ferry Farm, George Washington's boyhood home. Annual event.
Hours: 9:30am-3pm
Fee: Free
Ferry Farm, Kings Highway, Stafford County, VA
Contact: **Historic Kenmore**, 1201 Washington Avenue, Fredericksburg,

Remember that schedules do change.

VA 22401
Web: www.kenmore.org
(540)373-3381

Vienna
Near Washington, DC

July
🌱 Tour of Backyard Wildlife Habitats
A self-guided tour of beautiful certified
Backyard Wildlife Habitat landscapes in
northern Virginia. Special educational
demonstration and NWF naturalist at each
location. Contact sponsor for exact date.
Hours: 9am-5pm
Fee: $20 donation
National Wildlife Federation, 8925
Leesburg Pike, Vienna, VA 22184-0001
Web: www.nwf.org/habitats/
(703)790-4434

Virginia Beach

January 19-21
🌱 Virginia Flower & Garden Show ★★★
One of Virginia's premier flower & garden
shows. More than twenty major landscape
and floral display gardens, twenty seminars
and demonstrations by gardening experts,
over 180 vendors exhibiting garden-related
merchandise, children's activities, Virginia
Federation of Garden Club Shows and
European Flower Market. Sponsored by the
Professional Horticulture Conference of
Virginia.
Hours: 10am-9pm Fri-Sat; 10am-5pm Sun
Fee: $7; children under 12 free
Virginia Beach Pavilion, I-264, six blocks
from Virginia Beach oceanfront, Virginia
Beach, VA

Contact: **Virginia Flower & Garden Show**,
PO Box 10871, Norfolk, VA 23513
Web: www.virginiagardens.org
(757)853-0057

Warrenton

July 4
🌱 Piedmont Family Fair
Recommended for families. Celebrates the
rural economy, natural resources and history of the Virginia Piedmont region. Includes
nature walks, butterfly garden tours, flower
arranging seminars, farmers' market, fly
fishing on the lake, crafters, antique show,
vintage cars, sheepdog demonstrations,
jazz, country and bluegrass music, puppet
shows, petting zoo and good food. Annual
event.
Airlie Conference Center, Route 605
(Airlie Rd), Warrenton, VA
Contact: **Piedmont Environmental Council**,
45 Horner Street, PO Box 460, Warrenton,
VA 20186
Web: www.pec-va.org
(540)347-2334

Williamsburg

April 22-24
🌱 Colonial Williamsburg Garden Symposium
This year's theme, "Practical Gardening for
a Changing World." A symposium with lectures, tours, master classes, demonstration
classes and a faculty of well-known garden
lecturers, horticulturists and writers. Attracts
over 200 horticultural professionals and
home gardening enthusiasts annually.
Cosponsored by the American Horticultural

Be sure to check with the sponsor in advance.

Society. Annual event, now in its 55th year.
Fee: $168
Cascades Meeting Center, 104 Visitor
Center Drive, Williamsburg, VA
Contact: **Colonial Williamsburg**
Foundation, PO Box 1776, Williamsburg,
VA 23187-1776
Web: www.history.org
(800)603-0948

WEST VIRGINIA

Harpers Ferry

April 28-29
🌸 House & Garden Tour
A tour of eight to ten homes and gardens in
historic Berkeley and Jefferson Counties.
Tickets available in advance from sponsor
or at each house on days of tour. Annual
event, now in its 46th year.
Hours: 10am-5pm
Fee: $10 in advance; $12 day of tour; $5
children under 13
Shenandoah-Potomac Council of Garden
Clubs, PO Box 998, Harpers Ferry, WV
25425
Web: www.travelwv.com
Berkeley Co (800)498-2386 or (304)264-
8801 in WV; Jefferson Co (800)848-8687
or (304)535-2627 in WV

Shepherdstown

June 16
🌸 Historic Shepherdstown Garden Tour
A tour of private gardens in Shepherdstown,
most never on the tour before, plus a marketplace with flower vendors, garden crafts,
farmers market and a special children's tent
with activities for ages 6 to 12. English-style
tea available in the yard of historic Trinity
Episcopal Church for an additional fee.
Friends of Shepherdstown Public Library ,
West German Street, Shepherdstown,
WV 25443
Web: www.lib.shepherdstown.wv.us
(304)876-2783

White Sulphur Springs
7 miles from Lewisburg

April
🌸 Spring Violet Field Trip
Recommended for families. Show-me-hike
to find and identify 100-125 different flow-
ering species of wildflowers, including the
Bird's Foot violet native to this habitat. Six
tours available conducted by professional
guides. Annual event, now in its 35th year.
Contact sponsor for exact date.
Hours: 9am-5pm
Fee: Free
Greenbrier State Forest, White Sulphur
Springs, WV
Contact: **The American Violet Society**,
12602 Millbank Way, Herndon, VA 20170
Web: www.americanvioletsociety.org
(703)707-0049

FAR AWAY PLACES

See also garden tour specialists listed in the advertising pages.

Foreign Tours

February 1-21
❧ New Zealand & Tahiti Explorer
Starts in Auckland with visits to Orewa, Tiri Tiri Matangi, Rotorua, Christchurch, Fox Glacier, Queenstown, Te Anau, Stewart Island and ending in Dunedin. Includes visits to great New Zealand gardens and wildlife sanctuaries. Hikes of 2-4 miles over uneven terrain requiring moderate physical fitness. For more information, call (303)370-8051.
Denver Botanic Gardens, 909 York Street, Denver, CO 80206

February 9-19
❧ Travel to the Galapagos Islands
A tour to the Galapagos Islands, the remote volcanic archipelago that remains much as it was millions of years ago.
The Holden Arboretum, 9500 Sperry Road, Kirtland, OH 44094
Web: www.holdenarb.org
(440)256-1110

February 16-28
❧ Costa Rica Safari
Tented camp expedition with a 4 day and 3 night stay at Corcovado Lodge Tent Camp and stops at San Jose, Monteverde Cloud Forest Reserve and Arenal National Park. For information, call (800)942-6666 or see web site at www.haerttertravel.com.
American Horticultural Society, 7931 East Boulevard Drive, Alexandria, VA 22308
Web: www.ahs.org

March 4-17
❧ Gardens of the Great Houses & Ranches of Argentina
A tour inspired by the book on Argentina's great houses and gardens by author Mercedes Villegas de Lariviere. Visits Buenos Aires, Mar Del Plata, San Martin de los Andes and Llao Llao. For information, call (800)942-6666 or see web site at www.haerttertravel.com.
American Horticultural Society *See earlier listing in this section.*

March 16-27
❧ Gardens & Monuments of Sicily
A tour of Taormina, Syracuse, Agrigento and Palermo with visits to numerous private gardens and the residence of Daphne Phelps, author of A House in Sicily. For information, call (800)942-6666 or see web site at www.haerttertravel.com.
American Horticultural Society *See earlier listing in this section.*

March 21-30
❧ Costa Rica Family Adventure
A tour to Costa Rica especially designed for families. Includes visits to an active volcano, a canopy walk through the rain forest, a visit to a butterfly garden, the Children's Rainforest, and two days of relaxation on the Pacific coast.
The Holden Arboretum, 9500 Sperry Road, Kirtland, OH 44094
Web: www.holdenarb.org
(440)256-1110

May 2-16
🕮 Gardens of Coastal, Iberia, France & Belgium
An exploration of the west coast of Europe from Lisbon, Portugal to Dover, England on board the M/V Clipper Adventurer, with stops to visit gardens along the way. For information, call (800)942-6666 or see web site at www.haerttertravel.com.
American Horticultural Society See earlier listing in this section.

May 15-24
🕮 Gardens & Castles of England, France, Wales & Ireland
A tour from Dover, England to Dublin, Ireland on board the M/V Clipper Adventurer with stops for visits to private gardens along the way. For information, call (800)942-6666 or see web site at www.haerttertravel.com.
American Horticultural Society See earlier listing in this section.

May 19-26
🕮 The Great Gardens of England & The Royal Chelsea Flower Show
A tour of great English gardens, including Barnsley House, home garden of Rosemary Verey, Hidcote Manor Garden and Sissinghurst Castle, plus Member Day at the Chelsea Flower Show. For information, call (800)942-6666 or see web site at www.haerttertravel.com.
American Horticultural Society See earlier listing in this section.

May 20-30
🕮 Chelsea Flower Show & Garden Tour
A tour of private gardens in England, Wales

and Ireland, plus the Chelsea Flower Show. Hosted by Donna Dawson, Master Gardener. Stays at two special hotels, one in London and the other a manor house in the Cotswolds. Annual event, now in its 4th year.
Edmonton Horticultural Society, 1 Fenwick Crescent, St Albert, AB T8N 1W5
Web: www.ICanGarden.com/donnatour.htm
(780)460-1578

May 30 - June 13
🕮 World Bonsai Convention & Tour
A tour that includes the World Bonsai Convention in Munich as well as visits to important bonsai gardens in Austria, Italy and Switzerland. Originates in Atlanta, Georgia or other North American points by request.
Bonsai Clubs International, PO Box 8445, Metairie, LA 70011
Web: www.bonsai-bci.com
(504)832-8071

June 6-14
🕮 Gardens of the Italian Lakes
A tour that centers around Lake Maggiore and Lake Como with visits to exceptional private and public gardens. For information, call (800)942-6666 or see web site at www.haerttertravel.com.
American Horticultural Society See earlier listing in this section.

July 1-6
🕮 Scotland's Gardens Scheme Tour
Six-day tour in air conditioned coach to gardens in north of Scotland. Based for five nights in comfortable hotel with visits to two or three gardens each day. Great scenery and visits to private houses. Starts and

ends in Edinburgh.
Scotland's Gardens Scheme, 31 Castle Terrace, Edinburgh, EH1 2EL
E-mail: sgsoffice@aol.com
Fax: 011 44 131 229 0443

August 20 - September 6
Birds in the Bush Australia Tour
An introduction to the diversity of Australia's flora and wildlife from the rain forests and wetlands of Queensland and Kakadu National Park to the deserts of Alice Springs and Ayers Rock, the Great Barrier Reef and the southern coast of Victoria. Escorted by Allan Ridley and Toni Tully. For information, call (650)595-2090 or e-mail nzaus-tours@pacificpathways.com.
Strybing Arboretum & Botanical Gardens, Golden Gate Park, 9th Avenue & Lincoln Way, San Francisco, CA 94122
Web: www.strybing.org

September
Gardens of China
A tour of gardens in Beijing, Xian, Shexian, Mt. Huang, Hangzhou, Suzhou and Shanghai. For information, call (800)942-6666 or see web site at www.haerttertravel.com. Contact sponsor for exact dates.
American Horticultural Society *See earlier listing in this section.*

September 30 - October 12
A Deluxe Horticultural Safari to Kenya
Visits a range of climates from the temperate forests of Mt. Kenya to the semi-desert plains of the Masai Mara. Includes visits to Kenya's game parks with emphasis on horticultural highlights. Visits with some of the top Kenyan horticulturists. Deluxe accommodations in tented camps and lodges. Walking tours of short duration; uneven terrain can be expected. Optional extension to Tanzania, October 13-20, includes Lake Manyara National Park, Ngorongoro Crater and the Serengeti. For information, call (303)370-8051.
Denver Botanic Gardens, 909 York Street, Denver, CO 80206
Web: www.botanicgardens.org

October 1-18
Koala Bears and Blossoms
A 16-day tour of the gardens and natural wonders of Australia and New Zealand. Includes the Floriade show and Sydney Botanical Gardens.
Wichita Lawn, Flower & Garden Association, 9505 West Central, Suite 103, Wichita, KS 67212
Web: www.wichitagardenshow.com
(316)721-8740

October 15-19
Bonsai on Board
A cruise on board the Royal Caribbean Cruise Lines Majesty of the Seas the begins and ends in Miami with stops in Nassau, Coco Cay and Key West. Includes master workshops and demonstrations on board.
Bonsai Clubs International, PO Box 8445, Metairie, LA 70011
Web: www.bonsai-bci.com
(504)832-8071

October 25 - November 12
Gardens & Glaciers of New Zealand
Tour includes entry into exclusive private gardens, public gardens, scenic and cultural highlights and overnight cruise in Fiordland. Led by Dr. Ed Hasselkus, Professor Emeritus and Curator of the Longenecker Gardens at

the UW-Madison Arboretum. For information, call (650)595-2090 or email nzaustours@pacificpathways.com.
Friends of the UW Arboretum, 1207 Seminole Highway, Madison, WI 53711
Web: www.wisc.edu/arboretum/

Horticultural Events

AUSTRALIA

April
🌿 **Autumn Floral Festival**
A dazzling display of autumn color in these forty three hectare gardens in the heart of the Dandenong Ranges. Guided tours of the gardens as well as displays in the show hall. Annual event.
Rhododendron Gardens, The Georgian Road, Olinda, VIC 3788
Web: www.australia.com (Australian Tourist Commission)
+61 3 9816 1129

April
🌿 **Melbourne International Flower & Garden Show**
One of Australia's largest horticulture and floriculture shows held at the Royal Exhibition Building and in surrounding Carleton Gardens. Over 300 exhibitors, including floral designers, flower growers, landscape architects and designers, leading nurseries and florists. Annual event.
Royal Exhibition Centre & Carlton Gardens, Melbourne, VIC
Contact: **Nursery Industry Association of**

Victoria, PO Box 431, Caulfield East, 3145, Melbourne, VIC
Web: www.australia.com (Australian Tourist Commission)
+61 3 9576 0599

Spring
🌿 **Australia's Open Garden Scheme**★★★★
The organization sponsors open days at hundreds of private gardens country-wide, usually one weekend per location at peak bloom time. Proceeds benefit this nonprofit group which promotes gardens and gardening in Australia. Contact sponsor directly to obtain their guide which is available every year in August. Annual event.
Australia's Open Garden Scheme, Westport, New Gisborne, VIC 03438
Web: opengarden.abc.net.au
+61 (3) 5428 4557

May 10-13
🌿 **Festival of Gardens**
A major national show featuring dozens of miniature show gardens by some of Australia's leading landscape architects and designers. Annual event.
Darling Harbour, Sydney, NSW
Contact: **Festival of Gardens**, PO Box 526, Balgowlah 2093, NSW
E-mail: mdmgroup@one.net.au
61 2 9907 6575

August
🌿 **Nannup Flower & Garden Month**
A month of open gardens, talks, demonstrations, art exhibitions and antique auctions, plus thousands of daffodils planted throughout the gardens of Nannup. Annual

event.
Nannup Flower & Garden Month, 4
Brockman Street, Nannup, WA 6275
Web: www.australia.com (Australian Tourist
Commission)
+61 8 9756 1211

September 15 - October 14
☘ **Floriade**
Canberra's celebration of spring with over a
million annuals and bulbs blooming in spe-
cially designed flower beds on the shores of
Lake Hurley Griffin. For information, call
+61 02 6205 0044. Annual event.
Commonwealth Avenue Parks, Canberra,
ACT
Contact: **Australian Tourist Commission**,
Lev 4/80 William, Woolloomooloo, Sydney
2011, NSW
Web: www.australia.com (Australian Tourist
Commission)

October
☘ **Leura Gardens Festival**
Two weeks of open days at lovely private
gardens, with stunning mountain scenery
providing the backdrop for many of the gar-
dens. Shuttle bus tours available timed to
arrival of Sydney trains. Benefits the Blue
Mountains Hospital and attracts visitors
from all over the world. Annual event.
Contact sponsor for exact dates.
Leura Gardens Festival Committee, PO
Box 131, Leura, NSW 2780
Web: www.hermes.net.au/leuragardens/
+61 2 4784 1258

October
☘ **Kings Park Wildflower Festival**
One of Australia's largest and most varied
native plant displays and wildflower exhibitions. Educational and trade exhibits and
guided walks of Kings Park, a forty hectare
area of natural bush land in the heart of
Perth. Annual event.
Kings Park Botanical Gardens, Perth, WA
6000
Web: www.australia.com (Australian Tourist
Commission)
+61 8 9480 3600

October - November
☘ **Sunraysia Oasis Rose Festival**
A festival during peak bloom of the roses in
the Mildura region with garden tours, visits
to the Australian Botanic Inland Garden and
a program of keynote speakers. Annual
event.
Wildflower & Rose Festivals, 180-190
Deakin Avenue, Mildura, VIC 3500
Web: www.australia.com (Australian Tourist
Commission)
+61 3 5021 9138

BELGIUM

April 22 - May 8
☘ **Royal Greenhouses Open House**
The one time of the year that the Royal
Greenhouses of the Royal Palace at Laeken
are open to the public. Annual event.
Royal Palace, Laeken, Brussels
Contact: **Belgian Tourist Office**, 780 Third
Avenue, Suite 1501, New York, NY 10017
Web: www.visitbelgium.com
(212)758-8130

CARIBBEAN

January - December
✿ The Botanical Gardens of Nevis

A unique Garden located on the island of Nevis, just south of St. Kitts. Includes a rain forest conservatory with Mayan temple, ponds and flowing streams, and the Rose and Vine Gardens. Great views from the Tea House balcony.

The Botanical Garden of Nevis, PO Box 476, Montpelier Estates, St. John's Parish, Nevis
E-mail: JBrowne@gme-nevi.com
(869)469-3399

April 11, 25, May 2, 9, 16, 23
✿ Open House & Garden Tours in Bermuda

A tour of private gardens and National Trust gardens in Bermuda with a different residence open each day of the tour. For information, call (441)292-4912. Annual event.

Bermuda Department of Tourism, Lou Hammond & Associates, 39 East 51st Street, New York, NY 10022
Web: www.bermudatourism.com
1-800-BERMUDA

FRANCE

May 18-20, October 12-14
✿ Les Journees des Plants de Courson

A large exhibit and sale held twice a year on the grounds of the Domaine de Courson, a chateau near Paris. Includes more than 100 exhibitors and growers with their new introductions and unusual varieties. Annual event.

Domaine de Courson, Courson Monteloup
Contact: **Les Journees des Plants de**

Courson, Domaine de Courson 91680, Courson Monteloup
E-mail: courson@wanadoo.fr
011 33 1 64 58 9012

NEW ZEALAND

February
✿ Festival of Flowers

A community-wide week long garden festival with shows, activities, tours, exhibitions and food. Held in conjunction with the Festival of Romance, an arts and entertainment festival featuring music, theater and dance. Annual event.

Christchurch Canterbury Visitor Center, Christchurch
Web: www.summertimes.org.nz
E-mail: info@christchurchtourism.co.nz

October 19-26
✿ Rhododendron Festival

A week long festival featuring guest speakers and the best of the city's private and public gardens. Annual event.

Dunedin Rhododendron Festival, Dunedin
Web: www.cityofdunedin.com
+64 3474 3456

October 27 - November 5
✿ Taranaki Rhododendron Festival

Open garden days at more than 100 public and private gardens, plus seminars, tours and art exhibitions. Festival program available from the sponsor. Annual event.

Tourism Taranaki, Taranaki
Web: tipnet.taranaki.ac.nz/tourism
+64 6757 9909

November
☙ Southland's Festival of Gardens

A two-week festival with open days at some of Southland's finest gardens. Annual event.
Tourism Southland, Southland
E-mail: tourism@southnet.co.nz
+64 8007 33427

Mid November
☙ Greenworld Garden & ArtFEST

Open days at more than 90 gardens along the spectacular Pacific Coast Highway with works of art by local artists displayed and for sale in the gardens. Country craft fare and speakers. Annual event.
Greenworld Garden & ArtFEST, Bay of Plenty
Web: www.gardenandartfest.co.nz
+64 7543 1280

November 21-25
☙ Ellerslie Flower Show

One of the largest floral exhibitions in the southern hemisphere. Features hundreds of exhibits, thousands of colorful plants, garden art and market stalls. Held at a specially built site in the Auckland Regional Botanic Gardens with a spectacular backdrop of 200 year old Totara trees, beautiful native bush and a lake. Annual event.
Auckland Regional Botanic Gardens, Manurewa, Manukau City
Contact: **The Ellerslie Flower Show**, PO Box 6855, Wellesley Street, Auckland
Web: www.ellerlsieflowershow.com.nz
E-mail: mail@ellerslieflowershow.co.nz

THE NETHERLANDS

Late March - May
☙ Spring at the Keukenhof

A springtime display of as many as six million tulips and other flowering trees and plants, both outdoors and in several large greenhouses. Annual event.
Keukenhof Gardens, Lisse
Contact: **Netherlands Board of Tourism**, 355 Lexington Ave, New York, NY 10017
Web: www.goholland.com
(212)370-7360

August - September
☙ Zomerhof

A display of summer flowers including dahlias, lilies, gladioli, begonias and other summer flower, plus art exhibits. Annual event.
Keukenhof Gardens, Lisse
Contact: **Netherlands Board of Tourism**
See earlier listing in this section.

UNITED KINGDOM

Spring - Fall
☙ National Gardens Scheme★★★★

The "Yellow Book" (Gardens of England & Wales) lists open garden days at over 3,500 gardens, most of them private, in forty counties. The listings include descriptions of the gardens written by the owners, directions, hours and whether refreshments are available. All proceeds benefit charities. Order directly from their web site or from online book sellers. Available mid-February.

Annual event.
National Gardens Scheme, Hatchlands
Park, East Clandon, Guildford, Surrey GU4
7RT
Web: www.ngs.org.uk
011 44 148 321 1535

Spring - Fall
⚜ **Scotland's Gardens Scheme★★★★**
Over 350 gardens throughout Scotland
open for charity. Gardens of all sizes, most
offering teas, plant sales, gardening advice
and a warm welcome. Annual handbook
"Gardens of Scotland 2001" available mid-
February with directions and details.
Contact sponsor for ordering information.
Annual event, now in its 71st year.
Scotland's Gardens Scheme, 31 Castle
Terrace, Edinburgh EH1 2EL
E-mail: sgsoffice@aol.com
Fax: 011 44 131 229 0443

January - December
⚜ **Westminster Flower Shows**
Two-day flower shows held by the RHS
throughout the year featuring competitions
organized by various horticultural societies
and concluding with the RHS Christmas
Show in December. Contact sponsor for
exact dates.
The Royal Horticultural Hall, Vincent
Square & Greycoat Street, Westminster,
London
Contact: **The Royal Horticultural Society**,
80 Vincent Square, London SW1P 2PE
Web: www.rhs.org.uk
011 44 171 630 7422; 011 44 207 649-
1885 24-hr info

April 26-29
⚜ **Harrogate Spring Flower Show**
A famous show with displays from nurseries
and horticultural societies, including
Daffodil Society's Show and Early Season
Tulip Show. Annual event.
Great Yorkshire Showground, Harrogate,
North Yorkshire
Contact: **North of England Horticultural
Society**, 4a South Park Road, Harrogate,
North Yorkshire HG1 5QU
Web: www.flowershow.org.uk
011 44 142 356 1049

May 10-13
⚜ **Malvern Spring Garden Show**
A major British flower shows held against
the spectacular backdrop of the Malvern
Hills. Includes floral art, nearly 500 vendors'
booths, courtyard gardens, a specialist
society section and the RHS Advisory desk.
Organized jointly by the RHS and the Three
Counties Agricultural Society. Annual event.
Three Counties Showground, Malvern,
Worchestershire
Contact: **The Royal Horticultural Society**
See earlier listing in this section.
Web: www.rhs.org.uk

May 22-25
⚜ **Chelsea Flower Show ★★★★★**
The ultimate gardening event, held on the
grounds of The Royal Hospital, Chelsea,
London. Includes show gardens by the
world's leading designers, displays by specialist nurseries, top gardening products
and a range of conservation, education and
science displays. All tickets are sold in
advance. Annual event.
The Royal Hospital, Chelsea, London

Contact: **The Royal Horticultural Society**
See earlier listing in this section.
Web: www.rhs.org.uk

June 13-17
🌺 BBC Gardeners' World Live
Combines gardening showbiz with horticulture and features gardening celebrities from BBC Gardeners' World Live, the BBC Gardeners' World Magazine Theatre and a number of imaginative show gardens. Includes a RHS flower show. Annual event.
National Exhibition Centre, Birmingham
Contact: **The Royal Horticultural Society**
See earlier listing in this section.
Web: www.rhs.org.uk

June 21-24
🌺 Royal Highland Show
Held in Edinburgh. Annual event.
The Royal Horticultural Society *See earlier listing in this section.*
Web: www.rhs.org.uk

July 3-8
🌺 Hampton Court Palace Flower Show
Eight massive tents filled with flowers, many show gardens, water gardens, plants and many gardening accessories for sale, plus the Royal National Rose Society's British Rose Festival. Annual event.
Hampton Court, East Molesey, Surrey
Contact: **The Royal Horticultural Society**
See earlier listing in this section.
Web: www.rhs.org.uk

July 18-22
🌺 Tatton Park Flower Show
RHS show held on the grounds of one of England's great country estates. Annual event.

Grounds of the estate, Tatton Park
Contact: **The Royal Horticultural Society**
See earlier listing in this section.
Web: www.rhs.org.uk

July - August
🌺 Wisley Flower Shows
RHS shows held at the RHS Garden in Wisley. Annual event. Contact sponsor for exact dates.
The Royal Horticultural Society *See earlier listing in this section.*
Web: www.rhs.org.uk

September 14-16
🌺 Harrogate Autumn Flower Show
A major show with more than a dozen participating national horticultural societies and ninety nurseries. Annual event.
Great Yorkshire Showground, Harrogate, North Yorkshire
Contact: **North of England Horticultural Society**, 4a South Park Road, Harrogate, North Yorkshire HG1 5QU
Web: www.flowershow.org.uk
011 44 142 356 1049

September 18-19
🌺 Great Autumn Show
A seasonal show sponsored by the RHS. Annual event.
The Royal Horticultural Hall, Vincent Square & Greycoat Street, Westminster, London
Contact: **The Royal Horticultural Society**
See earlier listing in this section.
Web: www.rhs.org.uk

FLOWER & GARDEN SHOWS

MIDWEST

*For more information, see the **Midwest** edition of **The Garden Tourist 2001***

January 26 - February 4
🌹 Indianapolis Home Show
Indianapolis, IN
(800)395-1350 or (317)705-8719

February 3-4
🌹 Orchid Quest
Madison, WI
(608)831-2877

February 7-11
🌹 Minneapolis Home & Garden Show
Minneapolis, MN
(800)466-7469 or (952)933-3850

February 10-18
🌹 National Home & Garden Show★★★
Cleveland, OH
(216)529-1300

February 14-18
🌹 Des Moines Home & Garden Show
Des Moines, IA
(800)466-7469 or (952)933-3850

February 22-25
🌹 Michigan Home & Garden Show
Pontiac, MI
(616)530-1919

February 22-25
🌹 Youngstown Home & Garden Show

Youngstown, OH
(800)865-8859

February 24 - March 4
🌹 Fifth Third Bank Cincinnati Home & Garden Show★★★
Cincinnati, OH
(513)281-0022

February 24 - March 4
🌹 Columbus Dispatch Charities Home & Garden Show★★★
Columbus, OH
(614)461-5257

February 28 - March 4
🌹 Fort Wayne Home & Garden Show
Ft. Wayne, IN
(800)695-5288

February 28 - March 4
🌹 Wichita Lawn, Flower & Garden Show★★★
Wichita, KS
(316)721-8740

February 28 - March 4
🌹 St. Louis Builders Home & Garden Show
St. Louis, MO
(314)994-7700

March 1-4
🌹 West Michigan Home & Garden Show
Grand Rapids, MI
(616)530-1919

March 1-4
🌺 Akron-Canton Home & Garden Show
Akron, OH
(800)865-8859

March 9-11
🌺 Symphony in Bloom Lawn, Garden &
Flower Show
Davenport, IA
(319)322-0931

March 9-11
🌺 Dayton Home & Garden Show
Dayton, OH
(800)395-1350 or (317)705-8719

March 10-18
🌺 Chicago Flower & Garden Show★★★
Chicago, IL
(312)321-0077

March 10-18
🌺 Indiana Flower & Patio Show
Indianapolis, IN
(800)215-1700 or (317)576-9933

March 14-18
🌺 Canada Blooms!★★★★
Toronto, ON
(416)447-8655

March 15-18
🌺 Lansing Home & Garden Show
East Lansing, MI
(616)530-1919

March 16-18
🌺 International Home & Garden Show
Toronto, ON
(416)512-1305

March 16-18
🌺 Home, Garden & Leisure Living Show
Lincoln, NE
(402)473-4265

March 22-25
🌺 GMC Builders Home & Detroit Flower
Show
Detroit, MI
(248)737-4477

March 22-25
🌺 Kansas City Flower, Lawn & Garden Show
Kansas City, MO
(816)942-8800

March 23 - April 1
🌺 Realtors' Home & Garden Show
Milwaukee, WI
(414)778-4929

March 29 - April 1
🌺 DTE Energy Detroit International
Bloomfest★★★
Detroit, MI
(248)646-2990

March 29 - April 1
🌺 Ottawa Spring Home Show
Ottawa, ON
(613)241-2888

March 30 - April 1
🌺 Kitchener-Waterloo Home & Garden Show
Kitchener, ON
(519)741-2545 or (877)961-2999

March 30 - April 1
🌺 Springtime in Quinte Garden Show
Belleville, ON
(613)967-8520

March
Ontario Garden Show
Burlington, ON
(905)527-1158

April 5-8
Spring Home & Garden Show
Detroit, MI
(248)737-4477

April 6-15
National Home Show
Toronto, ON
(888)823-7469 or (416)385-1880

April 20-22
Chicago Botanic Garden Antiques & Garden Fair★★★
Chicago, IL
(847)835-5440

April 25-29
Cincinnati Flower Show★★★★
Cincinnati, OH
(513)872-5194

May 4-6
Orchard in Bloom Spring Gardening Show
Indianapolis, IN
(317)290-7673

June 2-3
Garden Fair
Green Bay, WI
(920)490-9457

November 8-17
The Royal Winter Garden at the Royal Agricultural Winter Fair★★★
Toronto, ON
(416)263-3400

NORTHEAST

*For more information, see the **Northeast** edition of **The Garden Tourist 2001***

February 1-4
Greater New York Home & Garden Show
Long Island, NY
(800)274-6948

February 9-11
Garden State Home Show
Somerset, NJ
(800)811-7469

February 15-18
Rhode Island Spring Flower & Garden Show★★★
Providence, RI
(401)272-0980

February 22-25
Connecticut Flower & Garden Show★★★
Hartford, CT
(860)529-2123

February 22-25
New Jersey Flower & Patio Show
Somerset, NJ
(800)215-1700 or (317)576-9933

February 22-25
Suburban Home & Garden Show
Philadelphia, PA
(800)756-5692 or (856)784-4774

February 23-25
Gramercy Garden Antiques Show
New York City, NY
(212)757-0915

March
🌹 Brookhaven Indoor Landscape & Garden Show
Holtsville, NY
(516)758-9664

March 2-4, 9-11
🌹 Maryland Home & Flower Show
Timonium, MD
(410)863-1180

March 4-11
🌹 The Philadelphia Flower Show★★★★★
Philadelphia, PA
(215)988-8800

March 9-11
🌹 Lehigh Valley Flower & Garden Show
Allentown, PA
(610)433-7541 or (610)437-6020

March 9-18
🌹 Duquesne Light Pittsburgh Home &
Garden Show★★★
Pittsburgh, PA
(412)922-4900 or (412)565-6000
(Convention Center)

March 10-18
🌹 Buffalo Home & Garden Show
Buffalo, NY
(800)274-6948

March 14-18
🌹 Portland Flower Show
Portland, ME
(207)774-1067

March 15-18
🌹 GardenScape★★★
Rochester, NY
(716)265-9018

March 15-18
🌹 Spring Flower & Garden Show★★★
Syracuse, NY
(315)592-9292

March 17-25
🌹 New England Spring Flower
Show★★★★
Boston, MA
(617)536-9280

March 17-18
🌹 Bucks Beautiful Garden Fair
Doylestown, PA
(215)348-3913

March 22-25
🌹 Rites of Spring Home & Garden Exhibition
Baltimore, MD
(410)554-2662

March 23-25
🌹 Capital District Garden & Flower Show★★★
Albany, NY
(518)356-6410 x418

March 29 - April 1
🌹 Washington Home & Garden Show
Washington, DC
(703)823-7960

March 29 - April 1
🌹 Central Massachusetts Spring Flower
Show★★★
Worcester, MA
(800)533-0229 or (508)832-3300

March 30 - April 1
🌹 Bangor Garden Show
Bangor, ME
(207)990-1201

March 30 - April 1
🌺 Breath of Spring Flower Show
Keene, NH
(603)352-2253

March 30 - April 1
🌺 The Southern New Jersey Home &
Garden Show
Atlantic City, NJ
(830)980-4078

April 5-8
🌺 Greater New York Orchid Show★★★
New York City, NY
(212)945-0505

April 19-22
🌺 Chester County Flower Show
West Chester, PA
(610)696-1309

April 27-29
🌺 Antique Garden Furniture Show & Sale
New York City, NY
(718)817-8700

May 4-6
🌺 Northeastern Pennsylvania Flower Show
Kingston, PA
(800)836-3413 or (570)457-8301

May 5-6
🌺 Gardenfest
Solomons, MD
(410)326-4640

October 19-21
🌺 Fall Maryland Home & Garden Show
Timonium, MD
(410)863-1180

SOUTHEAST
*For more information, see **Selected Events** section of this edition.*

January 19-21
🌺 Virginia Flower & Garden Show★★★
Virginia Beach, VA
(757)853-0057

January 19-21
🌺 The Low Country Living Home & Garden
Show
Savannah, GA
(830)980-4078

February 8-11
🌺 Atlanta Garden & Patio Show
Atlanta, GA
(770)998-9800

February 8-11
🌺 The Antiques & Garden Show of
Nashville★★★
Nashville, TN
(615)352-1282

February 16-18
🌺 Pensacola Home & Garden Show
Pensacola, FL
(800)226-3976 or (205)680-0234

February 21-25
🌺 Southeastern Flower Show★★★
Atlanta, GA
(404)888-5638

February 22-25
🌺 Jacksonville Home & Patio Show
Jacksonville, FL
(800)645-7798 or (904)730-3356

February 22-25
🌺 Dogwood Arts Festival House & Garden Show
Knoxville, TN
(865)637-4561 or (800)DOGWOOD

February 22-25
🌺 Maymont Flower & Garden Show★★★
Richmond, VA
(804)358-7166

February 23-25
🌺 Capital Home & Garden Show
Chantilly, VA
(800)274-6948

February 23-25
🌺 Palm Beach Tropical Flower & Garden Show★★★
West Palm Beach, FL
(561)655-5522

February 23-25
🌺 West Tennessee Lawn & Garden Show
Jackson, TN
(901)664-6161

February 24 - March 4
🌺 Southern Spring Show★★★
Charlotte, NC
(800)849-0248 or (704)376-6594

March 1-4
🌺 Nashville Lawn & Garden Show
Nashville, TN
(615)352-3863

March 2-4
🌺 Gulf Coast Home & Garden Show
Mobile, AL
(800)226-3976 or (205)680-0234

March 2-4
🌺 Miami International Orchid Show★★★
Miami, FL
(305)255-3656

March 8-11
🌺 Birmingham Home & Garden Show
Birmingham, AL
(800)226-3976 or (205)680-0234

March 8-11
🌺 The Home Garden & Remodeling Show
Louisville, KY
(502)429-6000

March 9-11
🌺 Kiwanis Garden Expo
Memphis, TN
(901)757-8788

March 15-18
🌺 Daytona Beach Garden Show★★★
Daytona Beach, FL
(904)252-1511

March 17-18
🌺 Metropolitan Miami Flower Show
Miami, FL
(305)271-0735

March 21-25
🌺 New Orleans Home & Garden Show
New Orleans, LA
(504)837-2700

March 22-25
🌺 Festival of Flowers
Mobile, AL
(334)639-2050

March 30 - April 1
🌹 Central Florida Home & Garden Show
Orlando, FL
(407)629-9242

April 6-8
🌹 Emerald Coast Flower & Garden Festival
Pensacola, FL
(850)432-6095 Mon, Wed, Fri 10am-3pm

April 7-8
🌹 Spring Garden Show
New Orleans, LA
(504)483-9386

April 27-29
🌹 Historic Abingdon Garden Faire
Abingdon, VA
(540)676-6309

April 28-29
🌹 Growin' in the Mountains Lawn & Garden Show
Fletcher, NC
(828)697-4891

September 21-23
🌹 Birmingham Fall Home Show
Birmingham, AL
(800)226-3976 or (205)680-0234

October 20-21
🌹 Fall Garden Show
New Orleans, LA
(504)483-9386

SOUTHWEST & ROCKIES

*For more information, see the **Southwest & Rockies** edition of **The Garden Tourist 2001***

January 19-21
🌹 Oklahoma City Home & Garden Show
Oklahoma City, OK
(800)527-7469 or (512)218-9118

January 19-21
🌹 Austin Home & Garden Show
Austin, TX
(800)527-7469 or (512)218-9118

February 1-4
🌹 Oklahoma Garden Festival★★★
Oklahoma City, OK
(405)528-2996

February 2-4
🌹 Houston Home & Garden Show
Houston, TX
(800)527-7469 or (512)218-9118

February 9-11
🌹 Texas Home & Garden Show
Houston, TX
(713)529-1616

February 9-11
🌹 San Antonio Home & Garden Show
San Antonio, TX
(800)527-7469 or (512)218-9118

February 10-18
🌹 Colorado Garden & Home Show
Denver, CO
(303)932-8100

February 15-17
🌹 Billings Home & Garden Show
Billings, MT
(406)245-0404

February 16-18
🌹 Spring Fort Worth Home & Garden Show
Fort Worth, TX
(713)529-1616

February 23-25
🌹 Neil Sperry's All Garden Show★★★
Dallas, TX
(800)752-4769

February 23-25
🌹 North Texas Spring Home Improvement
Show
Dallas, TX
(800)527-7469 or (512)218-9118

February 28 - March 4
🌹 Calgary Home & Garden Show
Calgary, AB
(403)209-3577 or (888)799-2545

March 2-4
🌹 GMC Phoenix Home Improvement &
Garden Show
Phoenix, AZ
(800)439-7550 or (602)277-4748

March 2-4
🌹 Arkansas Flower & Garden Show★★★
Little Rock, AR
(501)821-4000

March 2-4
🌹 Texas Home & Garden Show
Austin, TX
(713)529-1616

March 2-4
🌹 Dallas Home & Garden Show
Dallas, TX
(713)529-1616

March 2-4
🌹 Colorado Springs Home & Garden Show
Colorado Springs, CO
(800)811-7469

March 8-11
🌹 Salt Lake Tribune Spring Home & Garden
Festival
Salt Lake City, UT
(801)485-7399

March 14-18
🌹 Spring Home & Patio Show
Denver, CO
(303)892-6800

March 16-18
🌹 Texas Home & Garden Show
Fort Worth, TX
(713)529-1616

March 22-25
🌹 Edmonton Home & Garden Show
Edmonton, AB
(403)209-3577 or (888)799-2545

March 23-25
🌹 Arkansas River Valley Lawn & Garden
Show
Ft. Smith, AR
(501)785-5492

March 29 - April 1
🌹 Regina Home & Garden Show
Regina, SK
(306)569-2424

March 30 - April 1
🌹 Boise Flower & Garden Show
Boise, ID
(888)888-7631

March 30 - April 1
House, Flower & Garden Show
Austin, TX
(830)980-4078

April 20-22
Texas Home & Garden Show
San Antonio, TX
(713)529-1616

August 3-5
Houston House Beautiful Show
Houston, TX
(800)527-7469 or (512)218-9118

September 21-23
Fall Fort Worth Home & Garden Show
Fort Worth, TX
(713)529-1616

October 26-28
Arizona Fall Home Show
Phoenix, AZ
(800)439-7550 or (602)277-4748

WEST

For more information, see the ***West*** *edition of* ***The Garden Tourist 2001***

January 5-7
Puyallup Home, Flower & Garden Show
Puyallup, WA
(253)874-8711

January 19-21
South Bay Spring Home & Garden Show
Santa Clara, CA
(800)765-3976

January 31 - February 4
Tacoma Home & Garden Show
Tacoma, WA
(253)756-2121

February 2-4
Inland Valley Home & Garden Show
Ontario, CA
(800)442-7469 or (714)978-8888

February 7-11
Northwest Flower & Garden Show★★★★
Seattle, WA
(800)229-6311

February 8-11
Fascination of Orchids International Show & Sale★★★
Santa Ana, CA
(714)964-3265

February 16-18
Central Washington Home & Garden Show
Yakima, WA
(509)454-4006

February 21-25
Portland Home & Garden Show★★★
Portland, OR
(800)343--6973 or (503)246-8291

February 21-25
BC Home & Garden Show
Vancouver, BC
(800)633-8332 or (604)433-5121

February 22-25
Pacific Orchid Exposition★★★
San Francisco, CA
(415)546-9608

February 23-25
🌺 Yard, Garden & Patio Show
Portland, OR
(800)342-6401 or (503)653-8733

February 23-25
🌺 Regional Home & Garden Show
Pasco, WA
(509)735-2745

March 2-4
🌺 Peninsula Home & Garden Show
San Mateo, CA
(800)765-3976

March 2-4
🌺 San Diego Spring Home & Garden Show
Del Mar, CA
(858)552-8333

March 8-11
🌺 Fraser Valley Home & Garden Show
Abbotsford, BC
(800)633-8332 or (604)433-5121

March 21-25
🌺 San Francisco Flower & Garden
Show★★★
San Francisco, CA
(800)829-9751

March 23-25
🌺 Santa Barbara International Orchid
Show★★★
Santa Barbara, CA
(805)967-6331

April 20-22
🌺 San Jose Home & Garden Show
San Jose, CA
(800)765-3976

April 28-29
🌺 Green Scene Garden Show
Fullerton, CA
(714)278-3579

May 4-6
🌺 Central Coast Home & Garden Show
Lincoln City, OR
(541)994-3070

June 1-3
🌺 VanDusen Flower & Garden Show★★★
Vancouver, BC
(604)878-9274

July 24 - August 6
🌺 Sonoma County Fair
Santa Rosa, CA
(707)545-4200

August 18-26
🌺 Southern California Home & Garden Show
Anaheim, CA
(800)442-7469 or (714)978-8888

August 24-26
🌺 South Bay Fall Home & Garden Show
Santa Clara, CA
(800)765-3976

October 4-7
🌺 Fall Home & Garden Show
Portland, OR
(800)343--6973 or (503)246-8291

SECRET GARDEN GUIDES

Recommendations from local writers of little known, less frequented gardens that are well worth a visit

BATON ROUGE

When visiting Louisiana most people think of New Orleans and plantations, but the state capitol, Baton Rouge, is home to some wonderful gardens that are well worth a visit.

Start at the gardens of the **State Capitol**, designed to complement the state capitol building which was dedicated in 1932. E. A. McIlhenny, the designer of The Jungle Gardens of Avery Island, Louisiana, designed and planted this symetrical evergreen park with more than twelve thousand native Louisiana plants in the style of late 19th century English public gardens. In 1978, after many years of neglect, the 30-acre park and garden were restored to their former beauty and the site is now on the National Register of Historic Places. Boxwood-trimmed paths, a rose garden, annual beds, flowering shrubs and trees are beautifully maintained and provide a lovely place to stroll and visit. *Louisiana State Capitol*, Capitol Street, Baton Rouge, LA. Open daily, sunrise-sunset. Free. (225)219-4800

Louisiana State University's **Hilltop Arboretum** is the former property and work of Emory Smith and his wife to "get all of the beauty of the Louisiana woods into our own grounds." Emory Smith planned the garden to reflect the magnificence of a cathedral, with paths leading in every direction to settings of natural loveliness. He successfully planted wild azaleas, oak leaf hydrangeas and many other native trees and shrubs to create a wonderful setting that preserves the native character of the southern woodlands. The Arboretum is used by LSU as an outdoor laboratory but is also a special place to enjoy the atmosphere of natural calm and beauty. *Louisiana State University Hilltop Arboretum*, 11855 Highland Road, Baton Rouge, LA. Open daily, sunrise-sunset. Free. (225)767-6916

The **Laurens Henry Cohn Sr. Memorial Arboretum**, just north of Baton Rouge, was the estate of Maggie and Laurens Cohn, who planted the rural landscape surrounding their home with hundreds of trees and flowers and named the property *La Cuesta Enchantada*, the Enchanted Hill. This is a peaceful haven created by one man as a labor of love, which is now enjoyed by many. The Arboretum has since been further planted with many varieties of crape myrtle trees and an outstanding collection of Japanese maples. A large greenhouse has been added to house a tropical foliage collection. *Laurens Henry Cohn Sr. Memorial Arboretum*, Foster Road, Baton Rouge, LA. Open daily 8am-4:45pm. Free. (225)775-1006

The **Baton Rouge Botanic Garden**, established in 1994 in Independence Park, is a further extension of the Cohn Arboretum. Here you'll find a Rose Garden, Crape Myrtle Garden, Sensory Garden, Children's Forest and the Louisiana Iris Garden. *Baton Rouge Botanic Garden*, Independence Park, 7950 Independence Blvd, Baton Rouge, LA. Open daily, 7am-sundown. Free. (225)928-2270

Windrush Gardens, designed by the famous Steele Burden, is a must see in Baton Rouge. This garden was landscaped and developed by Burden as a place for reflection and meditation which he encouraged by placing benches and gazebos in quiet corners of the site. The design is a masterful combination of harmonizing green shapes, textures and peaceful colors. Burden's innovations in horticultural design - curved beds, naturalistic arrangements of flora, the use of lanterns and olive jars as accessories - are very much in evidence at Windrush. *Windrush Gardens*, Burden Research Plantation, Essen Lane, Baton Rouge, LA. Open daily, 8:30am-5pm. Admission charged. (225)765-2437

Outside the Baton Rouge area is another site of unusual interest to all nature lovers and feminists. If you can arrange to get there, Briarwood is well worth a visit.

Briarwood is a nature preserve in northern Louisiana, developed by Caroline Dormon, author, preservationist and America's first woman forester. Dormon's greatest achievement was the creation of the state's huge Kisatchie National Forest. But Briarwood was the woodland home where she and her sister made a garden of flora native to the southern United States, and where they planted her collection of Louisiana irises and other wetland plants. Today, visitors can follow Briarwood's trails and view the naturalist's own fine collection of Louisiana natives and rare southern plants and wildflowers in this 154-acre wild garden. *Briarwood*, Louisiana 9 (216 Caroline Dormon Road), Saline, LA. Open weekends in March, April, May, August and November, Sat 9am-5pm, Sun noon-5pm. Also open by appointment. Admission charged. (318)576-3379

Material for this article from Mary Fonseca's wonderful book, **Louisiana Gardens**, *with beautiful photographs by Steven Brooke. An absolute must for any garden tourist to Louisiana, virtual or actual. Mary is a Louisiana writer. Pelican Publishing Co., Inc, PO Box 3110, Gretna, LA 70053. http://ourworld.compuserve.com/homepages/mfonseca/index.htm 888-5PELICAN or 800-843-1724*

SAN FRANCISCO
by Beth Benjamin

In addition to all the great gardens in the San Francisco area, there are some off the beaten track gems that are well worth a visit. Here are some of my favorites.

Sierra Azui Nursery specializes in plants from the Mediterranean basin, South Africa, Australia, Chile, as well as California natives, and features species that are drought-tolerant and water conserving. It offers a beautiful and instructive 2-acre water-conserving demonstration garden, alive with birds, including many hummingbirds and butterflies, that is watered only once a month. *Sierra Azul Nursery*, 2660 East Lake Avenue, Watsonville. Open daily 9am-5:30pm. (831)763-0939

The **Berkely Horticultural Nursery** offers more than 2 acres of a wide variety of plants in a beautifully laid out nursery. Specializing in natives, aquatics and perennials, with strong specimens of maples, rhododendrons and camellias, Berkely Hort is a wonderful place to browse and get a sense of how the plants will look side by side. *Berkeley Horticultural Nursery*, 1310 mcGee Avenue, Berkely. Open 9am-5pm every day except Thursday. (510)526-4705

Maggie Wych of **Western Hills Rare Plants** continues the dream of the nursery's late founders, Marshall Olbrich and Lester Hawkins, to create both a world class garden and an eclectic nursery of unusual, rare and useful landscape plants. Set in the lovely countryside of Sonoma County, this extaordinary 3-acre nursery is an important destination for knowledgeable horticulturists from around the world. *Western Hills Rare Plants*, 16250 Coleman Valley Road, Occidental. Open Thurs-Sun 10am-4pm; by appointment only in December and January. (707)874-3731

Beth Benjamin, a partner at Renee's Garden, writes and gardens in Felton, California.

CONNECTICUT

For a small state, Connecticut seems to have many special nurseries that are well worth a side trip if you're in the New York area.

White Flower Farm in the foothills of the Berkshires in Litchfield is one of them. This well-known nursery has been family-owned since the late 1930s and includes numerous display gardens and production fields that are open to the public. If you have received a White Flower Farm catalog, you've had a taste of this beautiful site. Map for self-guided walking tours available. *White Flower Farm*, Route 63, Litchfield, CT. www.whiteflowerfarm.com (800)503-9624

Also in Litchfield is the **Litchfield Horticultural Center**, a local landscape design service, retail garden center and display garden. It includes great demonstration gardens like the woodland shade garden, a Zen garden, wetland, formal and watergarden, plus examples of driveway border treatment and mixed perennial borders.The Center includes more than 20 garden vignettes illustrating plant and design concepts that work well in the area. *Litchfield Horticultural Center*, 258 Beach Street,

Litchfield, CT. www.litchfieldhorticulture.com (860)567-3707
For lovers of rhododendrons and other woody plants, **Broken Arrow Nursery** is a good place to visit. This nursery started out 50 years ago as a grower of Christmas trees and for the last 16 years has been growing woodies and perennials, propagating most of the plants they sell. You can stroll through the nursery and surrounding landscape and see the many well established plantings as well as new varieties, visit the small pond, the grove of Christmas trees and enjoy the lovely view while the kids take a ride in the model train. *Broken Arrow Nursery*, 13 Broken Arrow Road, Hamden, CT. www.brokenarrownursery.com (203)288-1026

If you are an orchid freak or just love to look at these amazing plants, there's **J & L Orchids in Easton**. They hold three special events during the year that may entice you to make the visit, a summer sale at the end of June, a December Holiday Open House, and the annual January Thaw Sale at the beginning of the new year. *J & L Orchids*, 20 Sherwood Road, Easton, CT. www.orchidmall.com/jlorchid (203)261-8730

Thomaston is home to **Cricket Hill Garden** otherwise known as Peony Heaven. What makes this outstanding peony nursery even more special is its collection of Chinese tree peonies, the most extensive collection outside of China. Flowers usually bloom from mid May through early June. You can call them for bloom updates and then plan to go there and see the more than 200 varieties of peonies that grow in this unique 4-acre garden. *Cricket Hill Garden/Peony Heaven*, 670 Walnut Hill Road, Thomaston, CT. www.treepeony.com (860)283-1042

Logee's Greenhouses in Danielson is another nursery whose wonderful catalog will entice you to an on-site visit. The family has been growing and selling thousands of varieties of tropical and subtropical container and garden plants since 1892. There are seven greenhouses to wander through as you smell the fragrant air and get your fix of these exotics. *Logee's Greenhouses, Ltd*, 141 North Street, Danielson, CT. www.logees.com (888)330-8038

CHICAGO
by Susan Crawford

In addition to the renowned Chicago Botanic Garden in Glencoe, Chicago's two wonderful Conservatories and other well publicized sites, there are many lesser known garden spots in and around the city that are well worth a visit.

Two small gardens in the city are the **Lincoln Garden** behind the Chicago Historical Society and the **Rosenbaum Garden** on Oak Street just east of Michigan Avenue, both attractively planted and pleasant for a stroll or a picnic. If you are near Grant Park, visit the **Rose Gardens** north and south of the landmark Buckingham

Fountain, with beds of many varieties of modern roses.

On Michigan Avenue and LaSalle Street in downtown Chicago, island beds have been planted with an expert eye for color and scale. Anchored by stately grasses and perennials, with bulbs, annuals, vines and mums providing seasonal colors, these are spendid additions to the vibrancy of the urban scene.

On the Northwestern University Campus in nearby Evanston is the **Shakespeare Garden**. Designed by Jens Jensen in 1915 and maintained by the Evanston Garden Club, it represents a loose adaptation of the bard's planting list, with additions such as ornamental grasses. It offers a romantic and secluded sanctuary behind tall hedges.

Susan Crawford writes and gardens in Chicago.

MANHATTAN

If you are in New York City and feeling garden-deprived, you can satisfy your garden longings without leaving Manhattan.

In Greenwich Village stop by the **Jefferson Market Courthouse Garden**, right next to the Public Library housed in that wonderful building. This garden was created by local residents and is still maintained and tended by volunteers. It is open to the public on weekends, but you can look through the fence and get some idea of the peaceful, lush garden blooming in the heart of the Village.

In Soho try to look in on the **Liz Christy Garden**, a community garden which stretches from Second Avenue to Bowery on Houston Street. This exuberant garden has plots of vegetables, flowers, vines, shady trees, all sorts of horticultural expressions of the local artists and residents who grow and garden there.

Another community garden is found on the northern end of the spacious esplanade in Riverside Park. Enter the Park at Riverside Drive and 91st Street, go down the hill and up to the riot of color which has been planted down the center of the esplanade. The paving at the southern end of the esplanade is now being restored. When this project is finished the lovely shade garden will be replanted. Just south, along the Park's pathway, a local resident plants and maintains a perennial border.

Further uptown at the **Cathedral of St. John the Divine** on Amsterdam Avenue and West 100th Street, you can visit the Biblical Garden and the Hope Rose Garden. The latter is planted with David Austin roses.

Italy: Art, Architecture & Gardens
May 20 — June 2, 2001 / 12 nights

Including Florence, Sienna, Viterbo and Rome;
Villa Gamberaia, Boboli Gardens, Bomarzo,
Villa Lante, Villa Farnese, Villa d'Este, Ninfa,
Villa Aldobrandini, Castel Gandolfo and others.

Hampton Court Flower Show
& Gardens of England
June 27 — July 7, 2001 / 9 nights

Sissinghurst, Gardens of the Rose, Kew Gardens,
Beth Chatto's Garden, Hatfield House, Wisley,
David Austen's English Roses and others.

Copper Beech Garden Tours

Gardens in England & Europe

1010 Andrews Farm Road
Spartanburg, South Carolina 29302-2810
864-582-1498 tel/fax   LTMcHam@copper-beech.com

www.copper-beech.com

Experience The Natural Wonders

Heritage Herb Garden

The Ozark Folk Center is dedicated to preserving the mountain music and folk culture of the Ozark region. Many aspects of life in the Ozarks were, and still are, affected by the plant kingdom. The Heritage Herb Garden is made up of many unique areas throughout the park to preserve and interpret herbal lore. We hope the Heritage Herb Garden will enhance your visit to the Ozark Folk Center. For herbal enthusiasts, we offer structured seasonal workshops and seminars, design-your-own workshops and a Volunteer Garden Program. To participate in these or any other events, contact The Ozark Folk Center.

Herbs • Flowers • Kitchen • Butterfly

• **Yarb Garden** *(below Herb Cabin)* – This was our first herb garden. The granny woman or yarb doctor would have used many of the plants found here.

• **Native Plant Wildlife Garden** *(viewed from the Ozark Folk Center Restaurant)* – For birds, bees and butterflies, a rock pool graces the garden providing a water source for flora and fauna.

• **Terraced Garden** *(above Herb Cabin)* – Covering a hillside and root cellar, these plantings include native wildflowers, old-fashioned varieties and herbs of the world.

• **Herb Cabin** – In this demonstration and drying area, plant bunches are labeled as to name and traditional uses. Self-guided tour.

• **Organic Gardening** – Demonstrations throughout.

• **Garden For The Physically Challenged** *(across from the Smokehouse)* – These raised beds are planted with herbs that are to be touched, pinched and smelled, and can be accessed by a smooth pathway.

• **Kitchen Garden** *(entrance of the Skillet Restaurant)* – This demonstration garden provides fresh herbs, vegetables and edible flowers for Restaurant.

Hands-On Workshops • Weekend Seminars

Call for information on events, dates and workshops.

OZARK FOLK CENTER
P.O. Box 500 • Mountain View, AR 72560
870-269-3851
For lodge reservations: 1-800-264-FOLK
www.ozarkfolkcenter.com

Your Trees Deserve the Best of Care!

Caring for America's Trees Since 1907

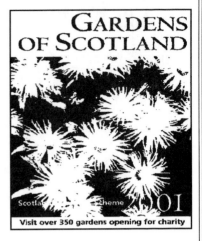

VISIT THE WILSON ROSE GARDEN
Stop Over
Interstate I-95, Exit 121
Wilson, North Carolina

The Wilson Rose Garden offers 140 varieties of roses, including 45 varieties of all America Award winners. A picnic area adjoins the garden.

DIRECTIONS: From I-95, take US 264 E. to Ward Blvd. Turn left at stoplight to Herring Avenue. Turn Left at light, go 1 mile. Rose Garden on the right.

WILSON ROSE GARDEN (No Admission)
For More Information contact the Wilson Visitors Bureau
1·800·497·7398
www.wilson-nc.com

CLASSIFIED ADS

Summer Garden Tour of Scotland - 9th Annual June 26 - July 12, 2001. Visit the private and famous gardens of Fife, Angus, Lothian, Aberdeenshire, Nairnshire, Sutherland and Ross regions! This tour includes Inverewe, Cawdor, Crathes, Falkland and the Royal Botanic Garden in Edinburgh. We accept VISA & MASTERCARD. The Garden Tours of Scotland, 26810 Country Road 98, Davis, CA 95616. For information, call (800)757-0404.

Golf, Gardens and Antiques of Scotland - 2nd Annual July 17 - August 2, 2001. Enjoy the glorious gardens of Fife, Angus, Sutherland and the Inverness area, the wonderful antiques, and the challenging golf courses of Scotland. This is a grand tour you will never forget! We accept VISA & MASTERCARD. The Garden Tours of Scotland, 26810 Country Road 98, Davis, CA 95616. For information, call (800)757-0404.

Irish Gardens Tour June 15-30, 2001. Bill Grant, leading tours since 1972, has arranged a fascinating program of visits to gardens throughout the Republic of Ireland and North Ireland. Our own coach and driver, stays in excellent hotels, and much more. For more information write or e-mail Port of Travel, 9515 Soquel Ave., Aptos, CA 95003. E-mail: grant@cruzio.com.

New Zealand - Australia Garden Tours Personal small group escorted tours or custom designed individual itineraries. Tours include entry into exclusive private gardens, public gardens, visits with plant specialists, scenic and cultural highlights, and overnight cruise. For info contact Pacific Pathways (650) 595-2090, e-mail nzaustours@pacificpathways.com or visit www.pacificpathways.com.

Wichita Lawn, Flower & Garden Show February 28 - March 4, 2001. Twelve incredible live gardens, HGTV celebrities, latest garden products, amateur & professional flower shows, fine art and crafts on a botanical theme, hourly seminars. "The Philadelphia Flower Show of the Midwest." For information, call (316) 721-8740, e-mail wlfandg@southwind.net or visit www.wichitagardenshow.com.

Koala Bears and Blossoms October 1-18, 2001. A 16-day tour of the gardens and natural wonders of Australia and New Zealand. Includes the Floriade show and Sydney Botanical Gardens. Sponsored by the Wichita Lawn, Flower & Garden Association, 9505 West Central, Suite 103, Wichita, KS 67212. For information, call (316) 721-8740, e-mail wlfandg@southwind.net or visit www.wichitagardenshow.com.

USEFUL BOOKS

The following is a list of some publications that we think gardeners on the go will find useful. If you know of a good guide that's not on this list, please let us know.

National Geographic Guide to America's Public Gardens *Mary Zuazua Jenkins, National Geographic Society, Washington, DC.* Beautiful photographs and detailed descriptions.

The Complete Guide to North American Gardens: The Northeast and The West Coast *William C. Mulligan, Little Brown & Co., New York, NY.* These two volumes cover gardens of major interest that are open to the public.

The Northwest Gardeners' Resource Directory *Stephanie Feeney, Cedarcroft Press, Bellingham, WA.* This wonderful compendium lists hundreds of horticultural resources in the northwest.

Gardener's On the Go!: Seattle *Stephanie Feeney, Cedarcroft Press, Bellingham, WA.* A must for visits to the Puget Sound area.

Garden Lover's Guide Series *Princeton Architectural Press.* Series includes guides to Italy, France, Germany, Britain, Spain and Portugal and is being expanded with guides to the U.S. and Canada.

Gardenwalks *Marina Harrison & Lucy D. Rosenfeld, Michael Kesend (publisher), New York, NY.* Gardens from Maine to Virginia, with some unusual and off-beat selections that are favorites of the authors.

The Adventurous Gardener *Ruah Donnelly, The Horticultural Press, Conway, MA.* A guide to New England's specialty nurseries and horticultural farms.

Louisians Gardens *Mary Fonseca with photographs by Steven Brooke, Pelican Publishing Co., Inc., Gretna, LA.* An absolute must for any garden tourist to Louisiana, virtual or actual.